1943

WHAT A YEAR TO BE BORN!

Written by
Robin Bennett-Freebairn and Joe Toussaint

Published by Emersive
www.whatayeartobeborn.com

What happened in 1943? We have a special affinity for the year we were born, but how much do we really know about it? This guide takes you through the highs and lows of an historic year in the midst of World War Two. The colour-coded chapters unlock a wealth of information that brings you closer to what life was like in this special year.

Contents

▶ Introduction

In 1943, the world was engulfed by war. Only a handful of nations declared themselves neutral. The United States had entered the war in December 1941, following the attack on Pearl Harbor, and had been actively fighting against the Axis powers, including Germany, Italy, and Japan, for over a year. On the Eastern Front, the Soviet Union continued to push back against the German invasion and had begun a counter-offensive. In July, the Soviets won a major victory at the Battle of Kursk, which was the largest tank battle in history and marked the turning point of the war on the Eastern Front. In the Pacific, the United States and its allies continued to fight against Japan, with significant battles taking place on the islands of Guadalcanal and Papua New Guinea. In June, the Allies won a crucial victory at the Battle of Midway, which was a turning point in the war in the Pacific. In Western Europe, the Allies began to gain ground against the Germans. In July, the Allies invaded Sicily, which led to the fall of the Italian government and their surrender. Significant progress was made in the war, with the Allies beginning to gain the upper hand against the Axis powers. However, the war would continue for another two years as Germany and Japan fiercely defended their homelands, with many more battles and casualties before it finally came to an end in 1945.

In Britain there was a slow return to normality in the towns and cities as the German Luftwaffe no longer had the capacity to bomb at will and could only carry out so-called tit-for-tat raids. This calm would not last as the Germans were developing the deadly and indiscriminate V1 and V2 rockets which would bring the return of aerial terror to the British people in 1944.

The year also saw the births of Mick Jagger and Keith Richards of the Rolling Stones and George Harrison of the Beatles. Popular names for girls born this year were Christine, Margaret and Patricia; for boys it was David, Michael and John. Competitive sport ground to a near halt. The Football League and F.A. Cup were suspended, although local and inter-service matches were arranged to boost morale. In horse racing the Derby went ahead at its temporary wartime home of Newmarket, the Grand National did not.

In January the film *Casablanca* received its nationwide release in the US. The musical *Oklahoma!* had its Broadway debut, while in Britain Irving Berlin's *This is the Army* played in London and Glasgow. Forces' sweetheart Vera Lynn appeared in two films *Rhythm Serenade* and *We'll Meet Again*. In literature, Roald Dahl published his first book, *The Gremlins*. Although John Steinbeck was widely tipped to win the Nobel Prize in Literature the prize was not awarded due to the war. Unsurprisingly, the Peace Prize was also withheld.

The Daily Headlines

No: 1263

Evening Edition

Price: Twopence

Thursday, January 14, 1943

PRIME MINISTER CHURCHILL AND PRESIDENT FRANKLIN D. ROOSEVELT ATTEND THE CASABLANCA CONFERENCE

The Daily Headlines

Price: Twopence

Friday, January 15, 1943

No: 1264

First Edition

CONSTRUCTION OF THE PENTAGON BUILDING IN ARLINGTON COUNTY, VIRGINIA IS COMPLETED

The Daily Headlines

Price: Twopence

Monday, May 17, 1943

No: 1385

Morning Edition

OPERATION CHASTISE DESTROYS THE EDERSEE DAM IN RAID USING BARNES WALLIS'S BOUNCING BOMBS

The Daily Headlines

No: 1400

First Edition

Price: Twopence

Tuesday, June 1, 1943

CELEBRATED ACTOR AND DIRECTOR LESLIE HOWARD DIES IN A PLANE CRASH OFF THE COAST OF SPAIN

Jan 1st   The New Year is heralded in with muted celebrations at home. The
           mood is further dampened by the introduction of rationing of bacon,
           butter and sugar.

Jan 2nd   The German Enigma Code is broken, giving the allies a significant
           strategic advantage in the war.

Jan 3rd   A twenty-room Hollywood mansion, owned by Bing Crosby, is destroyed
           by fire after a blaze broke out while the family were taking down
           their Christmas decorations. The fact that Crosby's White Christmas
           sits at No.1 in the Billboard charts softens the blow.

Jan 3rd   Britain and the United States announce the creation of the
           Combined Chief of Staff, a joint military command structure, to
           coordinate the Allied war effort.

Jan 6th   The British 8th Army, under the command of General Bernard
           Montgomery, begins the battle of Galaza in North Africa.

Jan 8th   Germany's elite Sixth Army is completely encircled in the Battle of
           Stalingrad. The Soviet Commander General Rokossovsky sends an
           ultimatum to his German counterpart, General Paulus. He gives
           Paulus until 10am the next morning to surrender. He promises food
           and medical attention, if the Germans give up.

Jan 9th   Knowing that the Soviet reassurances ring hollow, particularly
           after the suffering inflicted on the people of Stalingrad by the
           Nazis, Paulus allows the deadline to lapse.

Jan 10th   Operation Ring begins at 8.05am local time. It is the final assault on
           the German 6th Army. In a pincer movement, the five Soviet armies
           attack from all sides. 210,000 soldiers and 7,000 pieces of
           artillery are committed to the battle.

Jan 11th   British intelligence intercepts and decrypts the "Hofle Telegram", a
           report sent by SS major Hermann Hofle to his superior Adolf
           Eichmann. The telegram contains details of the murder of 1,274,166
           Polish Jews in death camps in 1942.

Jan 12th   The parents of the "Sullivan brothers", five men from Waterloo, Iowa,
           are informed that their sons had been missing in action since the
           sinking of USS Juneau in November. It is probably the heaviest blow
           suffered by a single family in American naval history.

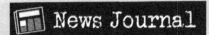
Jan 12th   Prime Minister Churchill flies to Morocco to meet US President Roosevelt to formulate plans for the next stage of the war.

Jan 15th   The Pentagon is officially opened, making it the largest office block in the world. The US now has the largest working space, to go with the tallest building, the Empire State Building.

Jan 16th   Berlin is bombed for the first time in over a year, as the RAF launches its heaviest raid ever on the German capital. 1,000 tons of bombs fall and fires are visible over 100 miles away.

Jan 17th   The Luftwaffe launch a night raid on London in a tit-for-tat action. It is the first raid since May 1941.

Jan 18th   The first Warsaw Ghetto Uprising begins. 200 SS troops storm the Ghetto but are driven back by a determined resistance. Deportations are temporarily halted.

Jan 18th   The Red Army of the Soviet Union breaks the 515 day siege of Leningrad. Russian General Georgy Zhukov is promoted to the rank of "Marshall of the Soviet Union".

Jan 18th   War Food Order No.1 comes into effect in America. It requires that white bread be enriched with iron, niacin, riboflavin and thiamine.

Jan 20th   A Luftwaffe daytime bombing raid leaves 41 children and 6 teachers dead at Sandhurst Road School located in the London suburb of Catford.

Jan 22nd   The townsfolk of Spearfish, South Dakota leave their house dressed for -20C weather (-4F) at 7.30am, only to see the temperature rise to a positively balmy 7C (45F) in the space of two minutes.

Jan 23rd   The all-time classic film Casablanca goes on general release in the US. Unbeknownst to the American public, their president is in Casablanca, Morocco at a key summit.

Jan 24th   Churchill and Roosevelt issue the Casablanca Declaration, insisting on the "unconditional surrender" of the Axis Powers - Germany, Japan and Italy.

Jan 30th   On the 10th anniversary of Hitlers assumption of power in Germany, he promotes General Paulus to the position of Field Marshal, with instructions to fight to the death in Russia.

Jan 31st   Field Marshal Paulus surrenders along with 90,000 German soldiers. He becomes the first German Field Marshal to surrender. The Soviet officers can scarcely believe their eyes.

Feb 1st   The 442nd Infantry Regiment whose soldiers are Americans of Japanese descent (Nisei) is created by an order of President Roosevelt. He proclaims that "No natural citizen of the United States should be denied the democratic right to exercise the responsibilities of his citizenship, regardless of ancestry. However most Nisei in the mainland US are still kept in internment camps.

Feb 3rd   The U.S. troop ship Dorchester is sunk 150 miles off the coast of Greenland. 605 of the 904 men on board perish.

Feb 6th   Lt. General Dwight D. Eisenhower is named commander of the Allied armies in North Africa. It is part of an agreement between Churchill and Roosevelt, but annoys General Montgomery, leader of the British and Commonwealth forces.

Feb 9th   U.S. President Roosevelt issues an order establishing a minimum wartime working week of 48 hours in cities that have labour shortages. However employees would receive "time and a half" for overtime.

Feb 10th   Imprisoned Mahatma Gandhi begins a 21-day hunger strike against British rule in India.

Feb 12th   William Morris, 1st Viscount Nuffield (of Morris Motors), creates the Nuffield Foundation, with a gift of £10 million.

Feb 16th   The port of Swansea, South Wales, suffers a third night of bombardment by the Luftwaffe. It leaves more that 200 dead and 400 injured.

Feb 17th   Russian composer and pianist Sergei Rachmaninoff gives his last concert in Knoxville, Tennessee. Deteriorating health forces him to abandon the rest of a nationwide tour of American universities.

Feb 22nd   Three members of the anti-Nazi "White Rose" student movement are executed in Germany. Although their campaign was non-violent they are condemned by the regime for their "treasonous activities."

Feb 22nd   A riot at Featherston POW camp in New Zealand leaves 48 Japanese prisoners and 1 New Zealand guard dead.

Feb 24th   A fire in the early hours at St Joseph's girls' orphanage in the city of Cavan, Ireland kills 35 girls between the ages of 4 and 15 and the 87-year-old school caretaker.

Feb 24th   The brand new British submarine HMS Vandal is lost shortly after launch in trials off the Scottish Isle of Arran. 37 crew are lost.

Feb 25th   Allied day/night bombing commences over Germany. The USAAF bomb in daylight hours, while the RAF bomb at night.

Feb 27th   Nancy Harkness Love becomes the first woman certified to fly a P-51 Mustang pursuit plane.

Mar 3rd   A panic during a suspected air raid leaves 62 children and 100 adults dead in the entrance way to Bethnal Green station in the East End of London.

Mar 4th   The 15th Academy Awards ceremony is held in Hollywood. Mrs Miniver wins best picture whilst Best Actress, London-born, Greer Garson delivers a six-minute acceptance speech.

Mar 6th   Fearful of the adulation being heaped upon the hero of Stalingrad, General Zhukov. Stalin promotes himself to the position of "Marshal of the Soviet Union." The communist party proclaim him to be "the greatest strategist of all times and all peoples." He is not.

Mar 7th   In the royal wedding of the year Prince Franz Joseph II of neutral Lichtenstein marries Countess Gina von Wildczek. The couple receive congratulations from both the Allied and the Axis powers.

Mar 10th   War torn Germany announces new rationing of non-essential goods, prohibiting the manufacture of suits, costumes, bath salts, and fireworks, and restricting telephone use and photography.

Mar 13th   German officer Henning von Tresckow arranges for a bottle of liquor to be delivered to Hitler. Instead of a bottle of alcohol, this thank you gift is in fact a bomb. All goes according to plan, until Hitler's plane takes off from Smolensk with the bottle on board, but it fails to explode due to a faulty detonator.

Mar 23rd   Parliamentary elections are held in Nazi occupied Denmark. Much to the displeasure of Adolph Hitler, the Social Democrats garner the most votes. Despite a campaign of intimidation, the Danish Nazi Party gain only 3% of the vote.

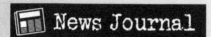

Mar 27th   The British escort carrier Dasher is destroyed in an explosion off the Firth of Clyde, Scotland, killing 379 of the crew of 528. An investigation concludes that the cause was a carelessly dropped cigarette.

Mar 29th   Food rationing begins in the United States. Pork, beef, lamb, canned fish, butter and cheese sales are restricted. Sales of poultry remain unaffected.

Mar 31st   The musical Oklahoma! by Rodgers and Hammerstein opens on Broadway.

Apr 1st   The RAF marks its 25th anniversary by presenting PM Churchill with honorary wings. "I am honoured to be accorded a place, albeit out of kindness, in that comradeship of the air which guards the life of our island and carries doom to tyrants, whether they flaunt themselves or burrow deep." he states.

Apr 4th   William Dyess escapes from a Japanese prisoner of war camp in the Philippines along with nine other men, and makes his way through the jungle to a ship that transports him to Australia. Once free, Dyess is able to reveal to the world the atrocities of the Bataan Death march that had taken place after U.S. and Philippine forces surrendered on 9th April 1942.

Apr 7th   The British government publishes a plan drawn up by John Maynard Keynes for a postwar economy. The plan proposed an international monetary fund which could help any nation out of temporary financial difficulties. In return, that country would have to adopt policies aimed at restoring stability.

Apr 12th   On Budget Day in the United Kingdom, Chancellor Sir Kingsley Wood announces that the war has cost Britain a total of £13 billion to date and was costing £15 million per day.

Apr 14th   Four inmates of Alcatraz Federal Penitentiary attempt to escape, making it to the water when the tower guards open fire on them. Two are killed and one hides until he is found three days later, but the body of the fourth, James Boarman, is never found.

Apr 16th   In Mexico, Ramon Mercader, a.k.a. Jacques Monard, is sentenced to 20 years in prison for the assassination of Russian Communist revolutionary Leon Trotsky with an ice pick in 1940.

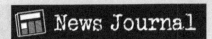
Apr 18th — America get their man. In an intelligence-led, targeted attack, Admiral Isoroku Yamamoto, the architect of the December 1941 attack on Pearl harbour is killed when the plane he is on is shot down by U.S. fighter pilot Thomas Lanphier Jr.

Apr 19th — Winston Churchill announces in Parliament that restrictions on the ringing of church bells throughout Britain is to be lifted as the threat of a German invasion has passed. The mood of the nation is lifted by the joyful chimes.

Apr 25th — Easter happens on its latest possible date. The last time it occurred on this date was in 1886, and the next time will be in 2038.

May 2nd — Operation Mincemeat, one of the greatest pieces of wartime deception, reaches fruition. A funeral in Spain is held for Major William Martin of the Royal Marines. Martin's body was washed ashore and on his person were detailed plans of a supposed invasion of Greece and Sardinia. Only Martin never existed and the body was that of a homeless Welshman, Glyndwr Michael The Germans fall for the deception and channel resources to the Italian island.

May 7th — Sex symbol Mae West, who had a life jacket named after her on account of her generous bust, is granted a divorce from her husband, Frank Szatkus. The couple have been separated for over thirty years.

May 9th — General Franco, the Fascist dictator of Spain, which remained nominally neutral during the war, gives a speech in favour of peace. He hopes that the Allies will forget the aid he received from Italy and Germany during the Spanish Civil War.

May 10th — To mark the tenth anniversary of Nazi book burnings in Germany, libraries across America fly their flags at half-mast.

May 13th — The North African Campaign comes to an end after almost three years of fierce fighting. British Field Marshal Sir Harold Alexander sends word to Churchill saying that "It is my duty to report that the Tunis campaign is over. All enemy resistance has ceased." More than 150,000 Germans and Italians become prisoners of war.

May 15th — The Irish steamship the Irish Oak is torpedoed and sunk in the Atlantic by a German U-boat despite being clearly marked as a neutral vessel.

May 16th   Operation Chastise, better known as the Dambusters Raid commences. RAF 617 squadron manage to breach two dams causing devastating flooding in the Ruhr valley.

May 18th   With an Allied invasion of Italy imminent, Pope Pius XII sends an appeal to U.S. President Roosevelt, asking that American bombers spare the destruction of Rome, noting that its "many treasured shrines of religion and art" were "the precious heritage not of one people but of all human and Christian civilisation".

May 19th   Churchill addresses a joint session of the United States Congress, reviewing the course of the war and reassuring his audience of Britain's dedication to its alliance with the USA. Churchill notes that "We will wage war at your side against Japan while there is breath in our bodies and while blood flows in our veins."

May 27th   Nazi censors in German-occupied Paris remove the painting of artists they deem decadent from the Galerie Nationale du Jeu de Paume . They then burn them in the museum's courtyard. Priceless works by Pablo Picasso, Max Ernst and Joan Miro are lost forever.

Jun 1st   English actor Leslie Howard is killed when the plane he is travelling in is shot down by German forces whilst in neutral Spain's airspace. One theory about the downing of the plane is that the Germans believed that Prime Minister Winston Churchill was on board, heading for a conference in Morocco.

Jun 14th   An American scientist, given the code name "Quantum" by Russia's KGB, meets with officials at the Soviet Embassy in Washington, DC. There he hands over classified scientific information about separating the isotope Uranium-235 from uranium. This is a key part of America's atomic bomb project.

Jun 16th   Charlie Chaplin elopes with Oona O'Neill, the daughter of playwright Eugene O'Neill; she is 36 years his junior. Her father disowns her.

Jun 18th   Ahead of the upcoming Allied invasion of Sicily, Winston Churchill discreetly removes Field Marshal Wavell and General Auchinleck from their positions of command in battlefield zones by appointing them Viceroy and Commander-in-Chief of India respectively.

Jun 23rd   A general election held in Ireland sees the incumbent Fianna Fáil party remain in power, but loses its overall majority.

Jun 24th   Trouble flares up between black American soldiers and white military police in Lancashire, England. One black soldier is killed in what became known as the Battle of Bamber Bridge.

Jun 29th   In advance of the Allied invasion of Sicily, General Eisenhower, the Allied Supreme Commander, sends a cablegram from North Africa requesting "on early convoy... shipment three million bottles Coca-Cola (filled) and complete equipment for bottling, washing, capping same quantity twice monthly", with the Coca-Cola Company sending "technical observers" to assist in the operation.

Jul 1st   The death sentence for treason for German-born American Max Stephan is commuted by U.S. President Roosevelt to life imprisonment, seven hours before Stephan was to be hanged. Stephan had been convicted of harbouring a German prisoner-of-war who had escaped from a POW camp in Canada.

Jul 3rd   The first residents arrive at the new town of Oak Ridge, Tennessee. The town has been constructed to house workers on the top secret atomic bomb project.

Jul 4th   The American Forces Radio Network is created to broadcast from 55 low-power transmitters near areas in the United Kingdom where American servicemen are stationed.

Jul 5th   The Battle of Kursk, the largest tank battle in history, begins when Germany launches an attack on the Soviet city of Kursk with 20 infantry divisions and 3,000 tanks.

Jul 8th   The Jamaican Labour party is founded by Alexander Bustamente.

Jul 9th   A Luftwaffe air raid kills 108 people, many of them children, in a cinema in the southern town of East Grinstead. Schoolchildren were packed in to the town's Whitehall Cinema to watch a Hopalong Cassidy film. Two bombs hit the building directly.

Jul 16th   Allied aircraft drop pamphlets over the Italian mainland with the message "Die for Mussolini and Hitler, or live for Italy and for civilisation". The message is backed up by Allied radio broadcasts.

Jul 16th   Batman and Robin are brought to film for the first time in a 15 instalment serial Lewis Wilson (26) appears as Bruce Wayne and Batman, while Douglas Croft (17) portrays Robin and Dick Grayson.

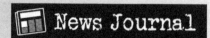

Jul 22nd George S. Patton's Seventh United States Army enters Palermo.

Jul 25th Italian "Duce" Benito Mussolini resigns along with the rest of his
        Fascist Party, thus bringing an end to over 17 years of dictatorial
        rule. He is arrested and driven away to face imprisonment.

Jul 26th American-born poet Ezra Pound is indicted for treason for making
        radio broadcasts from Italy for the Axis powers.

Jul 28th In the greatest single-day loss of life in wartime up to now, more
        than 30,000 residents of the German port city of Hamburg perish as
        British bombers carry out Operation Gomorrah during the night of
        July 27/28th.

Jul 30th The world's first jet-powered bomber airplane, the German Arado Ar
        234, makes its maiden flight.

Aug 2nd At 2am local time the US Navy patrol torpedo boat PT-109, with a
        crew of 13 commanded by Lieutenant John F. Kennedy, is rammed by
        the Japanese destroyer Amagiri while travelling through the
        Blackett Strait. Two of the crew are killed, while Kennedy and ten
        others swim 3 miles to a small uninhabited island.

Aug 4th British Prime Minister Winston Churchill and his cabinet ministers
        make what one commentator would call "one of his most important but
        least known decisions", electing not to ship British wheat to the
        colony in India, "thereby condemning hundreds of thousands, or
        possibly millions, of people to death by starvation". At the time,
        there was a famine in the Bengal province.

Aug 5th The battle of Kursk ends in defeat for the Nazis. The Germans have
        lost 70,000 men and 2,900 of their 3,000 tanks in the battle.

Aug 8th The United States Army bans the taking of photos at all beach
        resorts on the Atlantic Ocean, and even painting or sketching beach
        scenes, as part of defence of the eastern United States. Civilian
        violators could be barred from going to the coast, or even subjected
        to trial in a military court "for violating or conspiring to violate
        regulations".

Aug 22nd The identity of "Gertie from Berlin", who broadcast Nazi propaganda
        to English-speaking radio listeners, is revealed by the FBI to be
        Gertrude Hahn, an American citizen and native of Pittsburg. Miss
        Hahn moved her family to Berlin in 1938.

Aug 26th   Lord Mountbatten, Royal Navy Vice-Admiral and leader of the British Commandos in the Pacific War, is named by the Allies as the Supreme Allied Commander of Southeast Asia. Mountbatten is to conduct the Allied war effort against Japan in coordination with the Supreme Allied Commander in the Southwest Pacific operations, U.S. Army General Douglas MacArthur.

Aug 27th   The German rocket Henschel Hs 293 strikes and sinks HMS Egret, marking the first successful attack by a guided missile.

Aug 28th   The Danish government resigns rather than obey a German demand to prosecute suspected saboteurs in German military courts.

Aug 31st   The Grumman F6F Hellcat fighter is first used in combat, as groups of Hellcats take off from the aircraft carriers Yorktown, Independence and Essex. One commentator opined that "The introduction of the Hellcat may have been the most important event of the Pacific war".

Sept 2nd   Seweryn Klajnman, an 18-year-old Jewish inmate at the Treblinka Death Camp, leads an escape of 13 of his fellow prisoners. The group kills a Ukrainian SS guard, who is overseeing their work detail, with a crowbar. Klajnman then changes into the guard's uniform, and with rifle in hand and shouting orders, marches his group out of the camp's gates as if going to a new assignment.

Sept 3rd   The Italian mainland is invaded by the allies. The British commander General Montgomery sends the first British and Canadian troops across the Messina Strait, from Sicily to the southern tip of Italy. The British Eighth Army, 5th Division, and the Canadian 1st Division encounter little resistance after landing at Reggio di Calabria.

Sept 7th   As the German Army retreats from Ukraine, Heinrich Himmler issues a "scorched earth" (verbrannte Erde) order, with the goal to be "not one person remains, no cattle, no wheat, no railroad track... neither a house nor a mine which would not be destroyed for years... no well which would not be poisoned".

Sep 8th   Italy surrenders to the Allies. Over half of the 70,000 Allied prisoners-of-war are able to simply walk out of POW camps as their German guards flee to northern Italy.

Sep 10th   German forces invade Rome. The doors of St Peter's Basilica are blocked and the Vatican offers refuge to those fleeing the Nazis.

Sep 12ᵗʰ   In an audacious raid the German SS rescue Mussolini from his
            imprisonment at the Campo Imperiale Hotel, in the Abruzzi Mountains.
            Mussolini is taken to meet Hitler. The two greet each other as old
            friends, but the power balance has changed. Italy is all but lost.

Sep 15ᵗʰ   Three days after being freed from imprisonment by Germany, and
            seven weeks after his overthrow in July, Benito Mussolini is restored
            to leadership of Italy by the Nazi occupiers.

Sep 16ᵗʰ   The Salerno Mutiny: 700 soldiers of the British Army's X Corps refuse
            postings to new units in the Italian campaign. After negotiations,
            192 hold out and are sentenced to hard labour.

Sep 20ᵗʰ   The British de Havilland Vampire jet fighter makes its first flight,
            taking off from an airfield in Hatfield, Herts. Designer Geoffrey de
            Havilland is at the controls.

Sep 21ˢᵗ   American singer Kate Smith sings for 18 hours on CBS Radio
            appealing to her listeners to invest in U.S. war bonds. Her marathon
            performance is listened to by 85 million people and raises an
            astonishing $39 million dollars.

Oct 2ⁿᵈ   The Swedish Government issue a proclamation welcoming all refugees
            from neighbouring Denmark to their kingdom, which has remained
            neutral during the war.

Oct 5ᵗʰ   Adventurer, spy and journalist Theodore Morde meets with Franz von
            Papen, the German ambassador to Turkey. He attempts to persuade
            Papen to lead a coup against Hitler and install himself as leader.
            The meeting is not sanctioned by the US Government and is described
            as a "crazy attempt at personal diplomacy." Papen declines the offer.

Oct 7ᵗʰ   The children's film Lassie Come Home, starring the fictional Rough
            Collie Lassie, is released. British born child actor Roddy McDowall
            plays Lassie's companion.

Oct 12ᵗʰ   Neutral Portugal grant Britain the use of naval and air bases on
            the Azores, citing an agreement made 570 years previously. The
            Anglo-Portuguese treaty of 1373, is the oldest continuous treaty
            still in effect today.

Oct 17ᵗʰ   The Burma Railway, built using the forced labour of Asian civilians
            and Allied prisoners-of-war, is completed. It links Bangkok and
            Rangoon and provides a vital supply route for the Japanese.

 **News Journal**

Oct 18th   Perry Mason is first broadcast as a 15-minute long show on CBS radio, in America.

Oct 19th   African-American actor Paul Robeson makes his Broadway debut, portraying the title character in Shakespeare's Othello.

Oct 22nd   Circus performer Aloysius Peters, billed as "The Man With the Iron Neck" is killed when his signature stunt goes wrong at a rodeo in St. Louis, Missouri. Peters' act involved leaping from a trapeze bar with a noose around his neck made from an elastic rope. This time he got his timing wrong and his neck was broken.

Nov 5th   Four bombs are dropped on the Vatican City. Windows are broken at St. Peter's Basilica, but nobody is injured. A British RAF bomber near Rome was given permission to unload its bombs after developing engine trouble and released them "without quite knowing where it was".

Nov 8th   Radio Moscow broadcasts news from the newly liberated capital of the Ukraine, and reports that only one Jewish person has been left alive in Kyiv. Before the German invasion, the city's Jewish population had been 140,000.

Nov 12th   The final aerial bombardment of Darwin, the capital of Australia's Northern territory, takes place. Starting on February 19th, 1942, Darwin has been bombed on 63 different occasions by Japan before the tide of the war had turned.

Nov 14th   Little known stand-in conductor Leonard Bernstein, aged 25, brings the house down when he conducts the New York Philharmonic. The next morning the New York Times gives an excellent review of Bernstein's performance. Great things are predicted of the young man.

Nov 16th   Residents of the English Village of Tyneham in Dorset are given eviction notices. Signs posted in the village put the denizens on notice that they must leave by December 19th. None of them has a right to contest the order as they are all tenants of Nathaniel Bond, whose family own the properties. The War Department has acquired the area for use as a training ground in preparation for the D-Day landings.

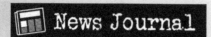

Nov 20th   British Fascist Leader Sir Oswald Moseley and his wife Diana Mitford are released from prison after three years of incarceration as a threat to national security. Home Secretary Herbert Morrison explains that the controversial release is on medical grounds. They are to stay under house arrest at Diana's sister's house.

Nov 26th   A 7.2 magnitude earthquake strikes Turkey along its Black sea coast. It leaves nearly 3,000 dead and destroys 25,000 buildings.

Dec 2nd   The Minister of Labour, Ernest Bevin, announces that one in ten men called up between the ages of 18 and 25 will be ordered to work in British coal mines. These conscripted miners would soon become known as the "Bevin Boys".

Dec 3rd   Edward R. Murrow delivers his classic "Orchestrated Hell" broadcast on CBS. He describes a night time bombing raid by RAF's 619 Squadron. Towards the end of his report he comments "Men die in the sky, while others are roasted alive in their cellars. Berlin last night was not a pretty sight."

Dec 4th   With the unemployment rate falling in America, due to increased wartime production, President FDR closes the Works Progress Administration, bringing a symbolic end to the Great Depression.

Dec 8th   The US President visits Malta and presents them with a scroll dedicated to its "people and defenders." It is further recognition of Malta's suffering and resilience during the war after Britain awarded the island the George Cross in April 1942.

Dec 13th   Italian scientist and resistance fighter Primo Levi is captured in Northern Italy. When his Nazi captors discover he is Jewish, he is sent to a camp for "processing".

Dec 13th   The first war crimes trial of the war begins in Kharov in the USSR. 3 German officers and a Russian collaborator are tried for "crimes and atrocities which have been, and are still being, committed by the German invaders." All four are found guilty and hanged.

Dec 17th   On the fortieth anniversary of the Wright Brothers' historic flight at Kitty Hawk, North Carolina, it is announced the Wright's airplane would be returned to the US from storage in England, and donated to the Smithsonian Institution. The Wrights had allowed the plane to leave the States after the Smithsonian had refused to recognise the brothers as the makers of the first flight.

Dec 22nd   Beatrix Potter, 77, Children's author, best known for her Peter
            Rabbit series of books, dies.

Dec 25th   In an unofficial Christmas Day truce the Allied bombardment of
            Berlin is temporarily halted. Similarly no German bombers attack
            Britain.

Dec 31st   British Deputy Prime Minister Clement Attlee broadcasts a New
            Year's Eve message to the people of the United Kingdom. Attlee
            recalled the events of the past year declaring:

"This year, for the first time, instead of Russian winter successes
being followed by a German advance in the summer, the Russian
attack has moved on successfully throughout the whole year. In the
Far East, the Japanese advance has been halted, and month by month
her outer ring of defences on the islands of the Pacific has been
penetrated. In the Battle of the Atlantic, after the difficult
months at the beginning of the year, the anti-U-boat war has gone in
our favour and Allied shipping resources have been steadily
growing. On the continent of Europe the activity of resistance
groups increasingly embarrassed the enemy, and tied down forces
which he urgently needs elsewhere. Cold and dark is the outlook for
Hitler and the Nazis. The passing year has been for their forces one
of continued retreat and of failure by land, sea and air. The hour of
reckoning has come, and they know that 1944 will mean for them only
heavier attacks. They still fight hard and skilfully, but the hope
of victory is dead in them, though some trust that a secret weapon
may enable them to postpone the inevitable."

Although optimistic he urged the British people not to be
complacent, stating:

"We can therefore close this year in a spirit of thankfulness for the
past and of hope and confidence for the future, but we must not
translate hope into relaxation or confidence into complacency. We
cannot tell what unsuspected trials may lie ahead of us: a war is
full of surprises. We do know that in 1944 the war will blaze up into
greater intensity than ever before, and that we must be prepared to
face heavier casualties. Nineteen-forty-four may be the victory
year; it will only be so if we continue to put forward our utmost
efforts, and if we allow nothing to divert us from our main purpose.

May I wish you all health, happiness and victory in the New Year."

Anthony Kenneth "Tony" Blackburn
born on 29th January 1943 in Guildford, Surrey, England

Tony Blackburn is a British radio DJ and television presenter, best known for his work on the BBC in the 1960s and 1970s. He was one of the original DJs on BBC Radio 1 when it launched in 1967 and remained with the station for over 50 years. Blackburn is known for his energetic and enthusiastic presenting style, and has presented many popular radio and television shows over the years, including *Pick of the Pops*, *The Blackburn Guide to Music* and *The Tony Blackburn Show*. In addition to his work on the BBC, Blackburn has also presented shows on other UK radio stations, including Capital Radio and Classic FM. In 2002 Blackburn was the first winner of TV's *I'm a Celebrity... Get Me Out Of Here!*

He has received numerous awards and accolades for his contributions to radio and television, including a lifetime achievement award from the Radio Academy in 2012. Blackburn has had a long and successful career in the media, and is well-respected for his knowledge and passion for music. He has remained popular with listeners and viewers for many years, and continues to be a popular and respected figure in the world of radio and television.

Most good pub quizzers will know that Tony Blackburn introduced the first song on Radio 1, *Flowers in the Rain* by The Move in 1967. However the first piece of music heard was Blackburn's introductory tune, *Theme One* by George Martin.

George Harrison
born on 25th February 1943 in Liverpool, England, UK

The son of a bus driver, George passed the 11-plus exam and was awarded a place at the Liverpool Institute, one of the city's leading grammar schools. There he met McCartney, who lived nearby, on the bus to school and the pair became best mates. When Paul linked up with John Lennon in *The Quarrymen* skiffle group, he tried to persuade the group to invite George to join. Lennon resisted, unwilling to have a 14 year-old kid in his band. He relented after hearing George's acoustic guitar rendition of Bill Justis' 1957 hit *Raunchy*. He realised that having a guitar soloist would allow the group to incorporate rock 'n roll material into its repertoire. Harrison's absorption in music took its toll on his academic career, and he left the Liverpool Institute in 1959 with only one exam pass, in art. However, the following year his musical career began in earnest when the re-named Beatles were booked to play for four months in a club in Hamburg's Reeperbahn. Although the trip was cut short when the 17-year-old Harrison was discovered to be under age. But probably his most important influence on the group concerned the new sound textures he introduced, particularly after linking up with sitar virtuoso Ravi Shankar.

The devastation caused by floods in Bangladesh in 1971 inspired Harrison to organise a major benefit concert in New York that was recorded and released as a live album the following year.

Sir John Major KG CH
born on 29th March 1943 in St Helier Hospital, London, UK

Major was the son of a circus performer. He left school at 16 to help support his family. He worked in a bank for several years, but always had a keen interest in Conservative politics. In 1974 he twice stood unsuccessfully for Parliament, before winning the seat of Huntingdon in Margaret Thatcher's landslide victory of 1979. His subsequent rise through the parliamentary party ranks was rapid, owing in no small part to the fact that he got on well with the PM. He became a junior minister in 1986 and Chief Secretary to the Treasury in 1987. By this stage, Thatcher, who had been in power for ten years, was making enemies in her own ranks. As one of the decreasing list of people she could trust, Major was appointed to the post of Foreign Secretary and three months later to the post of Chancellor of the Exchequer, replacing Geoffrey Howe and Nigel Lawson, respectively. When the two exiled big beasts of the party combined to oust Thatcher, Major was well placed to take over and he became Conservative Party leader and Prime Minister in November 1990. Often seen as a grey man, he was what the Tory party needed and he steadied the ship. His greatest achievement was to win the 1992 general election by campaigning with the aid of a megaphone and a soapbox. His 5-year tenure as PM was mired in economic strife and scandal and he was ousted in 1997.

Major is a keen follower of cricket and is honorary life vice-president of his beloved Surrey cricket club.

Eric Idle
born on 29th March 1943 in South Shields, County Durham, UK

Idle is an English comedian, actor, and writer best known for his work as a member of the Monty Python comedy troupe. He was born in 1943 in South Shields and began his career in entertainment as a writer and performer on the BBC Radio comedy show *I'm Sorry, I'll Read That Again*. He later joined the Monty Python team, writing and performing on the television series *Monty Python's Flying Circus* and in the Python films, including *Monty Python and the Holy Grail* and *Monty Python's Life of Brian*. Idle also wrote and starred in the hit Broadway musical *Spamalot*, which was based on the Python film *Monty Python and the Holy Grail*. He has also released several comedy albums, including *The Idle Race* and *Eric Idle Sings Monty Python*. In addition to his work with Monty Python, Idle has appeared in numerous films and television shows, including *Nuns on the Run*, *The Adventures of Baron Münchhausen* and *The Simpsons*. He has also written several books, including *The Road to Mars* and *The Greedy Bastard Diary*. Idle has received many awards throughout his career, including a BAFTA and a star on the Hollywood Walk of Fame for his work on *Spamalot*. He is also a Fellow of the British Academy of Songwriters, Composers and Authors and a Fellow of the Royal Society of Arts.

Idle was probably the most outgoing of the Python team and through his friendship with George Harrison, he was able to secure the money to make the film *Life of Brian*.

 Sir Michael Edward Palin KCMG CBE FRGS FRSGS
born on 5th May 1943 in Sheffield, England, UK

Michael studied Modern History at Oxford and after graduation became a writer, collaborating with Terry Jones to produce material for *The Frost Report* and other television programmes. By the time they'd written the prize winning TV series *Do Not Adjust Your Set* they had been joined by John Cleese and Eric Idle. Then, in 1969, Graham Chapman and Terry Gilliam joined them to form *Monty Python's Flying Circus*. While part of *Monty Python* during the 70's Michael was heavily involved with film spin-offs, books and specials based on the series but he also found time to write other material and appear in such productions as *Three Men in a Boat*. *Ripping Yarns* evolved from a half hour comedy script by Terry Jones and was a very successful TV series which won the Broadcasting Press Guild award as Best Comedy of 1977. Michael also wrote two plays with Terry Jones and co-starred in the film *Jabberwocky* directed by Terry Gilliam. The internationally successful film *Time Bandits* marked the start of Michael's association with Handmade Films which was followed by *The Missionary* which he wrote, produced and starred in. Prior to *A Private Function* he joined other Pythons in *The Meaning of Life*, then guest starred in *Brazil* directed by Terry Gilliam. *Around the World in 80 Days* was made in 1988, and marked the start of Michael Palin's career in making travelogues for BBC television. Subsequent programmes included *Full Circle* and *Pole to Pole*.

There was genuine tension towards the end of *Around the World in 80 Days* as Palin was behind schedule. But as in the Jules Verne book he made up time, arriving home in 79 days and 7 hours.

 Priscilla Maria Veronica White aka **Cilla Black** OBE
born on 27th May 1943 in Vauxhall, Liverpool, England, UK

The career of Cilla Black spanned more than 50 years and saw her develop from a 1960s pop starlet to TV royalty which led her to be affectionately known as "Our Cilla". Born in Liverpool as Priscilla Maria Veronica White, Black was brought up in a two-up, two-down house by a docker father and a mother who ran a market stall. Her stage name came about as a result of a misprint in a music paper. But she preferred the alternative, using it to launch a singing career which spawned many hits. Black's career started at the height of the Merseybeat era. She immersed herself in music while working as a cloakroom attendant at Liverpool's famous Cavern Club and serving coffee at another nightspot, the Zodiac. Black's big break came when John Lennon introduced her to Beatles' producer Brian Epstein. Overcome with nerves, she initially failed to impress. But she secured a contract when Epstein saw her again, and went on to have 19 consecutive UK top 40 hits. This included two consecutive number ones, *Anyone Who Had a Heart* and *You're My World* in 1964, and 11 top 10 entries. She went on to dominate Saturday prime time TV, hosting both *Surprise, Surprise* an ITV programme that aimed to make people's dreams come true and the matchmaking show *Blind Date*.

Mostly through her TV work Black was the highest paid female British entertainer from the late 1960s to the early 1990s.

Arthur Robert Ashe Jr.
born on 10th July 1943 in Richmond, Virginia, USA

Arthur Ashe was an American professional tennis player. He is considered one of the greatest players in the history of the sport, and was the first African American to win the men's singles title at the US Open and Wimbledon. Ashe turned professional in 1966 and quickly established himself as one of the best players in the world. He won his first major tournament, the US Open, in 1968, becoming the first African American to win a Grand Slam event. He went on to win the Australian Open in 1970 and Wimbledon in 1975, becoming the first and only African American to win the Wimbledon men's singles title. He was also known for his work off the court. He was an advocate for civil rights and used his platform as a professional athlete to speak out against racism and discrimination. He was also a vocal advocate for education, founding the Arthur Ashe Institute for Urban Health, which focuses on improving health outcomes for urban communities. In 1980, Ashe was diagnosed with a rare heart condition and was forced to retire from professional tennis. He continued to work on various philanthropic and humanitarian projects throughout the rest of his life, including the founding of the Arthur Ashe Foundation for the Defeat of AIDS. Ashe died from complications from AIDS in 1993, which he contracted from a blood transfusion. He was posthumously inducted into the International Tennis Hall of Fame in 1985.

When Nelson Mandela visited the USA after his release from prison in 1990 he was asked who he would like to meet first. He answered "why not Arthur Ashe?".

Robert Anthony De Niro Jr.
born on 17th August 1943 in New York City, USA

Robert De Niro is a highly acclaimed American actor, director and producer. He is considered one of the greatest actors of all time and has received numerous accolades for his performances. He has been nominated for the Academy Award for Best Actor/ Supporting Actor seven times and has won an award twice, for his roles in *The Godfather: Part II* and *Raging Bull*. He has also received several Golden Globe and BAFTA awards for his acting. De Niro began his career in the 1960s, but it wasn't until the 1970s that he gained widespread recognition for his performances. He starred in several iconic films during this decade, including *Mean Streets*, *The Godfather: Part II*, and *Taxi Driver*. De Niro has also had a successful career as a director and producer. He has directed several films, including *A Bronx Tale* and *The Good Shepherd*, and has produced many more, including *Jungle Fever* and *The Irishman*. He continues to be a major presence in Hollywood and has recently appeared in several high-profile films, including *Joker* and *The King of Comedy*.

The most iconic scene, in probably De Niro's finest role as Travis Bickle in Taxi Driver, was completely ad-libbed. Director Martin Scorsese locked De Niro in a room with just a gun and a mirror and the method actor came up trumps. "You talkin' to me? Is one of the greatest monologues in movie history.

Sir Michael Philip Jagger
born on 26th July 1943 in Dartford, Kent, England, UK

A Friendship Set in Stone - The Early Years

Mick Jagger and Keith Richards have known each other for seven decades. They grew up together in Dartford, a town in the county of Kent, England, and both attended Wentworth Primary School. "I can't remember when I didn't know him," Mick Jagger told Rolling Stone in 1995. "We lived one street away; his mother knew my mother, and we were at primary school together. We used to play together, and we weren't the closest friends, but we were friends."

Even beyond their primary school days, Jagger and Richards continued to orbit each other as kids. "We went to different schools when we were 11, but he went to a school which was really near where I used to live," Jagger told Rolling Stone. "But I always knew where he lived, because my mother would never lose contact with anybody, and she knew where they'd moved to. I used to see him coming home from his school, which was less than a mile away from where I lived."

One fateful day in October 1961, Mick Jagger and Keith Richards were at the Dartford Train Station preparing to head off to their respective colleges. Jagger was off to the London School of Economics, while Richards was heading for Sidcup Art College. Having lost touch for years, they bumped into each other and struck up a conversation. "I had these rhythm and blues records, which were very prized possessions because they weren't available in England then," Jagger told Rolling Stone. "And he said, 'Oh, yeah, these are really interesting.' That kind of did it. That's how it started, really".

From there, the pair kept in contact, often meeting to listen to records. Richards began picking up his guitar and playing it for Jagger. "So I said, 'Well, I sing, you know? And you play the guitar,'" Jagger recalled. "Very obvious stuff." They began collaborating, initially playing music as a pair, and later with two others in a band called Little Boy Blue and the Blue Boys in clubs around London.

On 12th July 1962, the Rolling Stones, named after a lyric in a Muddy Waters song, made their official debut. The line-up included Jagger and Richards, along with guitarist Brian Jones, keyboardist Ian Stewart, and drummer Mick Avory, who later joined The Kinks. The Rolling Stones went on to be possibly the greatest rock band in the world, releasing over 120 singles and 30 studio albums.

Surprisingly none of the Rolling Stone's albums feature in the top 60 albums sold in the UK. Instead Jagger and Richards made their wealth from touring. They have three of the top ten biggest grossing tours in history, (adjusted for inflation) namely the *Bigger Bang Tour* of 1985, the *Voodoo Lounge Tour* of 1994 and *The No Filter Tour* of 2017.

 ### Keith Richards
born on 18th December 1943 in Dartford, Kent, England, UK

Roberta Joan "Joni" Mitchell CC
born on 7th November 1943 in Fort Macleod, Alberta, Canada

Singer-songwriter Joni Mitchell was born Roberta Joan Anderson in Fort Macleod, Canada. At the age of 9, Mitchell contracted polio and it was during her recovery in the hospital that she began performing and singing to patients. After teaching herself how to play the guitar, she went to art college and quickly emerged as one of the leading folk performers of the late 1960s and '70s. At the beginning of her career, Mitchell's compositions were highly original and personal in their lyrical imagery. It was this style that first attracted attention among folk-music audiences in Toronto while she was still in her teens. She moved to the United States in the mid-1960s and in 1968 she recorded her first album, *Joni Mitchell*, produced by David Crosby. Other highly successful albums followed. She won her first Grammy Award (best folk performance) in 1969, for her second album, *Clouds*. Her third album, *Ladies of the Canyon*, was a mainstream success for the folk singer, becoming her first album to earn a gold disc, which included the hits *The Circle Game* and *Big Yellow Taxi*. It was during this time she was already starting to experiment with pop and rock genres. Her album *Court and Spark* (1974) signalled her foray into jazz and was lauded by critics; it ended up becoming her most commercially successful project to date.

Mitchell gave birth to a daughter in 1965 whom she gave up for adoption, In her song *Chinese Cafe* she alludes to the fact with the lyric "I bore her, but I could not raise her." The two were reunited in 1997.

Billie Jean King née Moffitt
born on 22nd November 1943 in Long Beach, California, USA

Billie Jean King is a former world No. 1 professional tennis player from the United States and considered one of the greatest female players of all time. King began playing tennis at a young age, quickly rising through the ranks and winning her first national junior championship at 14. She turned professional in 1968 and soon established herself as one of the top players in the world. In 1972, she founded the Women's Tennis Association and the Women's Sports Foundation, which promotes gender equality and supports female athletes. During her career she won 39 Grand Slam titles, including 12 singles, 16 women's doubles and 11 mixed doubles titles. She is best known for her historic defeat of Bobby Riggs in the 1973 "Battle of the Sexes" match, a landmark moment for the feminist movement that increased visibility and acceptance of women's tennis. The same year she became the first female athlete to earn over $100,000 in prize money in a year. King was also a trailblazer for women's rights and gender equality in sports. She has served as a mentor to many young female athletes and has been honoured with numerous awards, including the Presidential Medal of Freedom, awarded by President Obama in 2009.

In 1972, King became the first female athlete to be named *Sports Illustrated* Sportsman of the Year. In 1987, King was inducted into the International Tennis Hall of Fame. In 1990, *Life* magazine named her as one of the "100 Most Important Americans of the 20th Century".

James Douglas Morrison
born on 8th December 1943 in Melbourne, Florida, USA

Jim Morrison was the lead singer of the rock band The Doors. He was born in 1943 in Melbourne, Florida and died in 1971 in Paris, France at the age of 27, thus joining the "27 Club" whose members include Brian Jones, Jimi Hendrix and Janis Joplin among others. He was known for his charismatic stage presence, deep and powerful voice and poetic and provocative lyrics. He is considered one of the most iconic and influential frontmen in rock music history. Morrison formed The Doors in 1965 with Ray Manzarek, Robby Krieger and John Densmore. The band quickly gained popularity with their debut album, *The Doors*, which featured hit songs like *Break on Through (To the Other Side)* and *Light My Fire*. They went on to release several more successful albums, including *Strange Days*, *Waiting for the Sun* and *The Soft Parade*. Morrison's lyrics often dealt with themes of sex, drugs and rebellion, and his performances were regularly controversial and provocative. He was arrested multiple times for indecent exposure and public drunkenness, and his behaviour on stage was sometimes seen as wild and unpredictable. Despite this, he remained a popular and influential figure in the music industry until his death. After his death, Morrison's legend continued to grow, and he was posthumously inducted into the Rock and Roll Hall of Fame in 1993. His music and influence continue to be celebrated by fans and musicians alike.

Morrison's grave in Pere Lachaise cemetery has had to be fenced off to prevent cavorting couples from having fun on it.

Keith Floyd
born on 28th December 1943 in Sulhamstead, Berkshire, UK

Floyd was a British chef, restaurateur, and television personality known for his love of cooking and his charismatic on-screen presence. He began his career as a chef in the 1970s, working in a number of restaurants in the UK and France. In the 1980s, he began hosting his own cooking show, *Floyd on Fish* and later *Floyd on Food*, which aired on the BBC and were popular for their relaxed and unscripted style. He later hosted several other cooking shows, including *Keith Floyd's Mediterranean Cookery* and *Floyd Uncorked*. Floyd was known for his love of travel and his passion for discovering new ingredients and dishes from around the world. He often incorporated these into his cooking and was credited with introducing many people in the UK to unfamiliar ingredients and flavours. He also wrote several cookbooks, including *Floyd on France* and *Floyd on Italy*, which were well-received by critics and fans alike. Despite his success as a chef and television personality, Floyd struggled with alcoholism and personal issues throughout his life. He passed away in September 2009 at the age of 65. However, his legacy lives on through his cookbooks and TV shows, which continue to inspire and entertain audiences around the world. He is considered as one of the pioneers of TV cooking shows, who made cooking more entertaining and fun to watch. He cooked with a glass of wine in his hand and always had a good story to tell, which made him a much loved figure in the food world.

Floyd left us this mantra "Cooking is an art and patience a virtue... Careful shopping, fresh ingredients and an unhurried approach are nearly all you need".

 Sir Ben Kingsley born Krishna Pandit Bhanji
born on 31st December 1943 in Snainton, North Yorkshire, UK

Kingsley is recognised for playing a wide range of roles from Shakespearean tragedy and comedy through to tense dramas. He joined the Royal Shakespeare company in 1967 and made his Broadway debut with the company in 1971. Domestically most of his work was in television, even popping up in *Coronation Street* as Ron Jenkins in 1966. The 1970s saw his film debut in *Fear is the Key* (1973), but film work dried up until he was cast as Mohandas K. Gandhi (1982). To prepare for the role of the legendary pacifist Indian icon, he did extensive research, including practising yoga and adopting a vegetarian diet. The role was a huge success, helped by the fact that Kingsley bore more than a passing resemblance to Gandhi. It won him a best actor Oscar the following year. In the 90s he played a children's chess coach in *Searching for Bobby Fisher* and an accountant in *Schindler's List*. Kingsley continued to embrace diverse roles into the early 21st century. For his scene-stealing performance in *Sexy Beast* (2000), in which he played a terrifying psychopathic gangster, he earned a third Academy Award nomination. Kingsley garnered another Oscar nomination for his role as an Iranian immigrant being harassed by the former owner of his new home in *House of Sand and Fog* (2003).

In the role of Gandhi, Kingsley played the Indian leader between the ages of 23 and 78. Kingsley himself was 38.

Other Notable Births

 Janis Joplin
19th January 1943
Singer | Songwriter

 Joe Pesci
9th February 1943
Actor | Musician

 Graeme Garden
18th February 1943
Comedian | Actor

 Bobby Fischer
9th March 1943
Chess Champion

 Tony Christie
25th April 1943
Singer | Actor

Malcolm McDowell
13th June 1943
Actor | Producer

 Barry Manilow
17th June 1943
Singer | Songwriter

 Carly Simon
25th June 1943
Singer | Songwriter

 Roger Waters
6th September 1943
Singer | Songwriter

 Gloria Gaynor
7th September 1943
Singer

 Chevy Chase
8th October 1943
Comedian | Actor

 Catherine Deneuve
22nd October 1943
Actress | Model

 John Kerry
11th December 1943
Politician

 Chas Hodges
28th December 1943
Musician | Singer

 John Denver
31st December 1943
Singer | Songwriter

Nikola Tesla
died aged 86 on 7th January 1943 in New York City, USA

Despite his reputation as a child genius, engineer, inventor and physicist, Nikola Tesla never graduated from his university in Graz. He became addicted to gambling during his final year and, fearing humiliation, let his family believe he had drowned. In 1884 he travelled to the US and, after a brief stint working for Edison, began inventing for himself. After several failures and living in poverty, investors finally saw the value of his inventions. One of these was the AC induction motor, the patent that would make his fortune, being purchased by Westinghouse for $216,000. Freed from financial constraints, Tesla experimented at a furious rate. However, few of his ideas were taken up and his financial troubles returned. He then claimed to have invented a 'death ray' that would end all wars and a photographic technique for recording thoughts. This led to disbelief among investors. He was a living example of Aristotle's aphorism "No great mind has existed without a touch of madness."

Sergei Vasilyevich Rachmaninoff
died aged 69 on 28th March 1943 in Beverly Hills, California, USA

Rachmaninoff was a Russian composer, pianist, and conductor. However, he could do nothing right according to most of his contemporary critics and composers. As a person, he appeared somewhat cold and aloof - Stravinsky once called him "a six-and-a-half foot tall scowl". He left Russia for good after the 1917 Russian revolution, first heading to Helsinki and finally ending up in America. His student years had been nothing short of phenomenal. He consistently amazed his teachers with his jaw-dropping ability as a pianist and composer. In 1891 at the age of just 18, he created quite a storm with his *First Piano Concerto*, an incredibly accomplished work for a student. His masterpiece was surely the *Second Piano Concerto* from 1901. Its subsequent use in the film *Brief Encounter* has made it a constant favourite. In 1931 Rachmaninoff's music was officially banned in Russia as 'decadent' with the chilling warning: "This music is by a violent enemy of Soviet Russia: Rachmaninoff".

Martha Beatrice Webb, Baroness Passfield
died aged 85 on 30th April 1943 in Liphook, Hampshire, UK

Webb was a British social reformer, economist and political theorist of the late 19th and early 20th centuries. She was an active member of the Fabian Society and the London School of Economics. Webb is best known for her work on the issue of poverty and the labour movement. She wrote several books on these topics, including *Industrial Democracy* (1897) and *The Co-operative Movement in Great Britain* (1891). She was also a member of the Royal Commission on the Poor Laws and Relief of Distress (1905-1909), which led to the creation of the modern welfare state in Great Britain. She also played a significant role in the development of the Labour Party and the creation of the National Health Service. In addition, Webb was a strong advocate for women's rights and suffrage and was a member of the Women's Social and Political Union. Unlike her husband Sidney, she chose not to seek public office but instead sought to promote social change through her writings.

Leslie Howard Steiner better known as Leslie Howard
died aged 50 on 1st June 1943 at sea near Cedeira, Spain

Leslie Howard was an English actor and film director. He was born on 3rd April 1893 in London, England, and began his career as a stage actor in 1913. Howard appeared in many successful plays and musicals in the 1920s and 1930s, and made his film debut in 1922. He quickly became one of the most popular actors in Hollywood, starring in such films as *Outward Bound* (1930), *The Animal Kingdom* (1932) and *Berkeley Square* (1933). In addition to his acting career, Howard also directed several films, including *The First of the Few* (1942), which he also wrote and produced. During World War II, Howard served as a civilian pilot and made propaganda films for the British government. He died on June 1st when the plane he was travelling in was shot down by German forces. Despite his relatively short career, Howard left a lasting impact on the film industry and is remembered as one of the great actors of the early 20th century.

Thomas Wright "Fats" Waller
died aged 39 on 15th December 1943 in Kansas City, Missouri, USA

Fats Waller was a jazz pianist, organist, composer and bandleader from New York City. He was a prominent figure in the Harlem Renaissance of the 1920s and 1930s, and is considered one of the greatest jazz musicians of the era. Waller's style was characterised by his virtuosic piano playing, as well as his comedic stage presence and sense of humour. He composed and recorded hundreds of songs throughout his career, many of which became jazz standards, such as *Ain't Misbehavin'* and *Honeysuckle Rose*. He also made numerous appearances in films and on radio programmes, cementing his status as a popular entertainer. Waller also led his own band, Fats Waller and His Rhythm, which was known for its tight arrangements and innovative jazz rhythms. He performed with many other prominent jazz musicians of the time, including Louis Armstrong and Benny Goodman. He was inducted into the Songwriters Hall of Fame in 1970 and the Big Band and Jazz Hall of Fame in 1981.

Helen Beatrix Potter
died aged 77 on 22nd December 1943 near Sawrey, Cumbria, UK

Potter was an English author, illustrator, natural scientist and conservationist best known for her children's books, which featured animal characters such as Peter Rabbit. Born in 1866 in London, Potter was educated at home and had a love of nature and animals from a young age. She began illustrating and writing stories, eventually publishing her first book, *The Tale of Peter Rabbit*, in 1902. The book was a success and was followed by several more, including *The Tale of Squirrel Nutkin*, *The Tailor of Gloucester* and *The Tale of Benjamin Bunny*. Potter's books have been translated into many languages and remain popular to this day. In addition to her writing and illustration work, Potter was also a farmer and conservationist, working to preserve the land and animals of the Lake District where she lived. Her legacy is best seen in the land she bought and then bequeathed to the nation. Tarn Hows, near Hawkshead, is perhaps the finest example of this.

The Coins We Used

28 years before decimalisation, we used the system of **pounds**, **shillings** and **pence** commonly represented using the symbols **£sd**. The £ symbol evolved over many years from the letter **L** which derives from the Latin word *libra*, meaning a pound of money. Although **s** is the first letter of the word shilling, the use of the letter derives from the Latin word *solidus* which means coin. The curious use of the letter **d** for pennies also has a Latin origin from the word *denarius* meaning containing ten. Unlike the decimal system based on multiples of 10, the pre-decimal system was based on multiples of 12. There were 12 pennies to a shilling and 240 pennies to a pound. This meant there were 20 shillings to the pound. In 1943 there were 9 coins in circulation with evocative names that still permeate our language today.

Farthing = ¼ d
In use to 1961

With 4 farthings to a penny, these smallest of coins featured a smooth edge and a wren on the reverse. *He hasn't got two farthings to rub together* was a popular expression to describe someone poor.

Halfpenny = ½ d
In use to 1969

Commonly known as the *ha'penny* it is was the only word in the English language with a silent 'f'. Since 1937 the coin featured Sir Francis Drake's ship The Golden Hind. The popular pub game *Shove Ha'penny* features 5 halfpennies.

Penny = 1d
In use to 1971

Pre 1860 the penny was a large copper coin. This is why bicycles with a large front wheel were nicknamed Penny Farthings. Popular expressions using the penny include *ten a penny* and *penny for your thoughts*.

Threepence = 3d
In use to 1971

These 12-sided coins were commonly known as *thruppence* or *thrupenny bits*. The silver versions known as *joeys* were often hidden in Christmas puddings making an exciting find for the lucky children who discovered them.

Sixpence = 6d
In use to 1980

These silver coins reputedly brought good luck. Sixpences were placed in bride's shoes as a wedding gesture. Known as benders, they could easily be bent. *Going on a bender* derived from drinking all day in pubs with sixpence.

Shilling = 1/-
In use to 1990

First minted in the reign of Henry VII as a testoon, the shilling was latterly commonly known as a bob. *Taking the king's shilling* meant enrolling in the army whilst *A few bob short of a pound* describes someone a bit mad.

Florin = 2/-
In use to 1992

The florin was Britain's first decimal coin in response to calls in the mid 19th century for decimal coinage to be introduced. As 2 *bob* the florin was worth 1/10th of a pound. After decimalisation in 1971 florins became worth 10 pence.

Half Crown = 2/6
In use to 1969

Half crowns were originally struck in gold in the reign of Henry VIII. The first silver half crowns were issued under Edward VII in 1557. Surviving for over 450 years, the Half Crown was one of the most successful coins of all time.

Crown = 5/-
In use to present day

The British crown is a heavy silver coin. Rarely spent crowns are often minted for commemorative purposes. After decimalisation a crown was worth 25p until 1990 when their face value was changed to £5.

The average annual salary in the UK in 1943 was approximately:

£200-£280

The price of the average house would be approximately 3-4x the average annual salary. Depending on where you were in the country this meant the price of a typical 1930's 3-bedroom semi-detached house would be in the region of:

£720 -£960

Although commercial car production effectively ceased during the war, prices remained virtually static pre and post war. This example of a Morris 8 Series E launched in 1938 would cost:

£175

The Utility Radio or Wartime Civilian Receiver was a standardised radio developed by British radio manufacturers during the war. It cost:

£12 3s 4d

The maximum retail price of bread per lb (including National Wheatmeal Bread) is:

2d

A dozen Grade II eggs would cost a maximum of:

2s 3d

Working Life in the Factory

In 1943 the factory largely meant one place, the munitions factory. Virtually all industrial production had been turned over to producing instruments of war. As large numbers of men had gone abroad to do their bit, it was once more the role of women to stand in and undertake work that would usually be the domain of men. Women were recruited with posters reminding them that the lives of their husbands, lovers and brothers depended on their work. During the war over one million women worked in munitions factories and while the financial rewards were relatively high, so were the risks.

The factories operated using production lines and often very little training was given. The women were quickly shown what to do and then did it. Shells had to be loaded with hot TNT dispensed by a machine akin to a cement mixer and then a detonator had to be attached. This work was arduous, boring and repetitive but required great powers of concentration as the filling of every shell was fraught with risk. Another big danger came from the fact that a direct hit from an enemy bomb might obliterate the whole factory killing those inside. For fear that morale would be damaged, most accidents and fatalities were not widely reported. Aside from the risks of explosion, the materials the workers handled were extremely toxic and any contact with the face would require immediate medical attention. Apart from the physical danger, the chemicals turned many women's hair orange and their skin yellow.

Hours were long and the factories were open around the clock; sometimes the women were required to work eighty-plus hour weeks. The pay was however good, though not anywhere equal to a man's salary. It was the first time in British history that ordinary women had so much disposable income. Their wages were spent on almost any luxury item they could get their hands on, be it cosmetics, stockings or handbags. Black marketeers had a field day. The women were cash rich and time poor and when given time off partied hard like there was no tomorrow, in the knowledge that for many there might not be one. Britain could not have emerged victorious without the help of these women who worked all hours to supply our armed forces. After a long running campaign, in 2012, 18 of the munitions workers finally got to lay a wreath at the cenotaph on Remembrance Day to honour their fallen comrades.

Drilling components in a munitions factory

GECO Munitions factory, Scarborough

Clocking off at the end of a long day

Working Life on the Farm

Farming in the UK during the Second World War underwent a complete upheaval. It was essential that the government controlled what farmers grew and what livestock they kept in order to maximise nutritional output. For example, the government sought to place limits on the production of meat as this was considered wasteful and encouraged growing of vegetables rich in carbohydrates such as potatoes.

Women's Land Army harvesting beets

Food that had been imported from the Empire before the war was no longer available and American food aid had only just begun to arrive. The Ministry of Agriculture also instigated a programme of culling animals classed as pests. Deer, rabbits, birds and rats were killed in large numbers. Most would end up as part of a hearty stew, but hopefully not the rats.

Naval ratings lifting their parsnip crop

1943 was a good year to be a farmer, there was increased mechanisation and food inflation was rife, the Government also handed out generous subsidies. Day-to-day life on the farm also changed markedly from before the war. Many men had joined the armed forces and there was a shortage of labour. At first many women signed up to join the Women's Land Army, helping to greatly increase food production. However, by the end of 1943, the attraction of farm work had faded. Women were paid only half the rate of men doing the same often backbreaking work. Living conditions were often appalling and the cities from which most of the women came were now safer as Germany's ability to bomb them had been undermined.

Weaning a calf on a farm in Dartington

The year saw what had been a voluntary service being replaced by conscription. The unemployed from the cities, conscientious objectors and prisoners of war were also put to work on the farm. The male farm workers who remained at home, especially the skilled ones, saw their pay increase markedly; this was done with the full backing of the Government as they were considered essential to the war effort.

Membership of the National Union of Farmworkers trebled during the war, giving the workers even greater bargaining power.

Harvesting flax

Office Life

In 1943 office life was arcane, both in the equipment used and in the social structures it imposed. Men held nearly all of the managerial posts and women's roles were mainly secretarial. It was even the case that those, both men and women, who worked in the civil service had to ask permission of their boss if they wanted to marry. Some who were refused had no option but to leave the service if they wanted to continue with their nuptials.

The two main means of communication were back then the telephone and typed letters, often transcribed from shorthand notes. Although the photocopier had been invented before the war it was in the early stage of development and had not made its way from America. Copies had to be made using carbon paper fitted between plain sheets. There was a limit to how many could be produced and the secretaries had to bang hard on the keys of the manual typewriter to make them legible, slowing down their work and creating an almighty din in the office. Computers did exist but these were used mainly to decipher enemy codes, no-one had yet foreseen their use in the office.

One group of office workers who had the most demanding though probably the most rewarding job were those assigned to Prime Minister Winston Churchill. As well as being a great war leader Churchill was also an idiosyncratic character. There are stories of him giving dictation from the bath. The one male secretary was allowed in the room, but if he was unavailable the women would have to pin their ears to the door as he barked out his messages. He would also like to keep his staff on their toes saying things like "get me Ian from Sussex on the phone", knowing full well that the first time the secretary heard the order they would have no idea what he was talking about. In reality the word secretary hardly described their roles. They were chauffeurs, international conference organisers, pet-sitters, purchaser of cigars, champagne and even worms for his fish. The modern day term for the roles would be personal assistant or office manager but these were different times. Despite the travails of working in the War Office all his staff spoke fondly of working there and in those most demanding of times enjoyed being part of Churchill's team.

19 year old typist Iris Joyce

The Telephone Service central control room

Winston Churchill at 10 Downing Street

A Snapshot of Life in the Army

On their way to fight in Tunisia in 1943 a group of soldiers started their long journey on the 9th December 1942 on the pier alongside the troop ship Cameronia as it sat berthed in the King George V Dock in Glasgow. Most of the recruits that would board it had not even ventured on a ferry to Skye before, and now they were going to a place that they could scarcely imagine, North Africa.

As the troops struggled up the steep gang planks, laden with kit to board the ship, there was no fanfare. Instead they were greeted by a solitary stern military police officer who handed them a slip of paper identifying which area of the ship each man was to be assigned to.

On board conditions were cramped and while there were no good places to be, there were plenty of bad ones. The men spent their days squeezed around tables, whilst at night they would sleep in hammocks, an experience new to most of them. The worst berths were near the propellers making sleep almost impossible. Instructions were barked at the soldiers and there was a lot to remember.

Kit, bedding and equipment had to be stored tidily and away from passageways and nothing should be thrown overboard for fear of alerting German submarines. One thing that did make it overboard however was the contents of the soldiers' stomachs as most on board suffered terrible seasickness.

Life on board was extremely regimented. Times that a soldier could smoke, wash, eat, parade and sleep were all regulated. Drinking water was at a premium and the water used to brush ones teeth would be recycled in order to have a shave. In British waters the weather was dreich, as they say in Scotland, but after a few days it improved. The now sunny weather raised the spirits of all on board, but this was tempered by the realisation that better visibility made them vulnerable to enemy attack.

After what seemed like an eternity at sea, but in reality was only a number of days, the coast of North Africa came into view. An alien landscape. The soldiers on board the TS Cameronia were about to swap one misery for another.

The Troop Ship Cameronia

Crowded conditions on board a troop ship

Troops looking out on arrival in port

Soldiers disembark using a landing craft

Relaxing in the living room of their suburban London home, the Chillingworth family gather around the fire. Whilst Sydney reads the newspaper, his wife Hilda is darning a sock. Their daughter, Jill, is knitting a scarf whilst her brother, Jeremy, is playing with his toy castle.

In Eltham, South-East London Mr. and Mrs. Suter are enjoying some fresh bread and a pot of tea at breakfast time in their family home.

Mrs. Day is carefully sorting the cinders from the ash from last night's fire. She will re-use the cinders in the grate for today's fire whilst the ash will be saved to help fertilise the garden.

Back in the Chillingworth house, it is 8 o'clock in the morning and Mrs Chillingworth is helping her two children get ready for school. Sydney, her husband, has been working on night duty at the local fire station as he works for the National Fire Service.

As it gets dark seven-year-old Doreen Buckner draws the curtains at home in London. To ensure no light escapes into the night sky every house also has blackout curtains across every window.

With so many essential supplies rationed The Ministry of Food encouraged people to cook their entire meal in the oven to minimise how much fuel they used.

Furniture

Make do and mend were the watchwords of life during the austerity of the Second World War. Due to enemy disruption of British supplies from its Empire, everyday materials that were once in abundant supply, were now scarce. For most buying from new was no longer an option. The only new furniture produced during the war came under a strict government rationing scheme. In 1941 the Board of Trade designed a collection of furniture that could be produced cheaply and was of simple design. In 1942 Sir Hugh Dalton, President of the Board of Trade announced their aim was: "To secure the production of furniture of sound construction, in simple but agreeable designs and at reasonable prices." The furniture went on general sale in 1943. The original catalogue contained 30 pieces, their design being overseen by leading furniture designer Gordon Russell. Every piece had to comply with Utility Scheme standards and was stamped CC41 (Controlled Commodity 1941).

Only newly-weds or those whose homes had suffered significant bomb damage could apply for a permit to buy the furniture. A points system was put in place, each household would receive up to 30 points. Two chairs were worth 12 points and a sideboard 8, leaving little room for anything else. Very soon after the arrival of this furniture a small and illegal cottage industry grew up where people would adorn the plain furniture and attempt to sell it at higher prices. After the war, utility furniture slowly fell out of favour as people became able to afford a more decorative style. It has however gone through periodic revivals. Today, furniture which bears the mark CC41 does well at auction.

Woolton Pie

Woolton pie, named after Frederick Marquis 1st Lord Woolton, was a pastry dish of vegetables suggested to the British people when shortages, particularly of meat, made other dishes hard to prepare. Though it was created by the head chef at the Savoy Hotel in London, it was rather an austere product and soon fell out of favour after the war.

Recipe

The ingredients can be varied according to which vegetables are in season.

For the filling

1lb carrots
1lb swede
1lb potatoes
1lb cauliflower
1 heaped teaspoon vegetable extract
1 heaped tablespoon oatmeal
A handful of parsley

For the pastry

3oz of fat, lard, margarine or butter
5oz wheatmeal or plain flour
1 teaspoon baking powder
4oz cooled, cooked potatoes
Salt to taste

Method: Place all the filling ingredients, save the parsley, into a pan with just enough water to cover. Cook on a medium to high heat and stir frequently to stop the mixture sticking. After 10 minutes the vegetables should yield to a knife still yet be intact. Place in a pie dish, sprinkle with parsley and allow to cool in the dish. For the pastry: beat the fat with a fork until soft and then work in the flour, potato, baking powder and salt through a sieve. Work the mixture by hand into a pliable dough and then roll out. Cover the vegetable mixture with the pastry and place in a moderate oven until the pastry is nicely golden. Serve with brown gravy.

Carrot Cake

One recipe that did not only survive the war, but thrived, was carrot cake. Strict sugar rationing meant that other sources of sweetness had to be found and whilst many root vegetables such as swedes and parsnips were used, the carrot was favoured for its texture and colour. One big difference between the cake of 1943 and that of today is that you would have been extremely lucky to find it topped with icing.

Recipe

Ingredients

6oz plain flour
1 level teaspoon baking powder
3oz fat, lard, margarine or butter (or a mixture of each)
3oz oatmeal
1½ tablespoons sugar
1 grated medium sized carrot (2 if sugar is unavailable)
1 powdered egg (reconstituted) or 1 fresh egg
1 dessert spoon syrup
Water to mix

Method: Rub the fat into the flour, add the dry ingredients and the carrots and mix, stirring thoroughly. Add the egg and syrup and stir, add sufficient water to form a fairly stiff mixture. Transfer to a greased tin and bake in a moderate oven. After about 40 minutes test the cake with a knife, if it comes out clean the cake is cooked. Allow to cool on a baking rack and then serve. Store in a tin and eat within one week.

Holidays

Before the war foreign holidays for the people of Britain were the domain of the wealthy, but from 1939 this was no longer an option even for those who could afford them. In other parts of the world, like North America, holidays were possible although made more difficult as resources such as petrol and trains were being diverted to the war effort. By 1943 the British Government's "Holidays at Home" scheme was in full swing. Its aim was to dissuade people from making long trips by highlighting previously neglected attractions of people's home towns. Take-up by local authorities was patchy. Edinburgh council was one organisation that backed the scheme wholeheartedly. Picnics, games, music, singing, dancing and raffles were organised, all against the magnificent backdrop of Arthur's Seat. Though no match for a real holiday people could make believe and look forward to a time when actual holidays were possible.

Arthur's Seat overlooking Edinburgh

Blackpool

Blackpool stood out as a place where people could holiday with some semblance of normality. In fact the town thrived during the war. It had much going for it, accommodation was in plentiful supply as were the people to fill it. Many civil servants had relocated from London, the town saw tens of thousands of airman billeted there and American service personnel were stationed at nearby Warton. Women from nearby factories and those who worked the land also descended on Blackpool to enjoy any precious leave they were granted. Blackpool also had the advantage of being almost totally safe from enemy bombing – during the war there was only one attack resulting in fatalities. The town was of little strategic importance and the Luftwaffe were reluctant to damage the iconic Blackpool Tower as it provided a good navigational aid. Plays that would have normally been performed in London's West End moved north to Blackpool. Many of the plays had a war theme including Tolstoy's *War and Peace* which premiered in 1943. All in all if you had a choice of anywhere to take a break in Britain it would have been Blackpool, Lancashire's party town. The Americans brought with them money and luxuries boosting the local economy, while the arrival of thespians from London brought an air of culture. In 1943 the whole town had a holiday camp feel allowing people to let their hair down and recharge the batteries for the often daunting tasks that lay ahead.

Blackpool Tower

Crime

During the war while most of the population pulled together to defeat the enemy, a small but not inconsiderable section of the population seemed to be pulling in the opposite direction. From the commencement of the war in 1939 until its conclusion six years later, crime rose across the board in the UK by 57%. Bomb damaged London provided rich pickings for those willing to stoop so low and there were even cases of emergency service workers helping themselves. On August 3rd 1943, Gerald Elphinstone-Roe became another "client" of lead executioner Albert Pierrepoint, when he was hanged at London's Pentonville prison for the murder of his wife Elsie. Gangland crime was rife in London as traditional cockney mobsters fought battles with Maltese, Jewish and Italian gangs. The presence of so many soldiers from home and abroad had led to a lucrative vice trade and the gangs were willing to use extreme violence to gain control over it. Rationing led to a flourishing black market and the gangs were there to exploit every opportunity. The fact that the capital saw many police officers join the army did not help. There were several jewellery heists carried out by a gang led by North London villain Billy Hill. Forgery and theft of ration books and clothing coupons were rife up and down the country and criminals found a ready market with people desperate to supplement their meagre rations. The Government books and coupons were so rudimentary they were very easy to forge and few people were ever prosecuted for producing or handling them. Conmen also took advantage. For example, a contractor conspired with a Hammersmith clerk of works to pass air-raid shelters as safe when they were anything but. Many people died as a result of this shoddy workmanship and manslaughter charges followed. When the Government planned the evacuation of children from our cities at the beginning of the War they hadn't bargained for the fact that nearly half would remain. By 1943 few schools were open and many children lived feral lives leading to a large increase in anti-social behaviour. Some of the increase in crime can, however, be put down to the fact that defence regulations brought in during the war meant that there were now more laws to break. Some seemingly minor infringements were punished harshly. An engine tester in Coventry was sentenced to three months' hard labour in 1943 after taking 10 days off without permission when he got married. Similarly, two women from King's Norton, in Birmingham, were fined in January 1943 for refusing to do war work.

A police sergeant in Wotton-under-Edge

A police motorcyclist calls the station

Helping an international soldier

As can be seen from these photographs, despite raw materials being in short supply, wartime "austerity" fashions were not drab. Here is a purple, green and mauve dress designed by well-known fashion designer Norman Hartnell. The dress cost 7 clothing coupons.

This scarlet wool Utility frock was designed by the fashion label Dorville and sold by John Lewis and Co. Ltd. It cost 11 coupons and 60/-.

This mustard-coloured wool Spectator dress cost 11 coupons. It is paired with a dark-coloured turban, a popular head wear item. The ensemble is finished with a handbag with large metal clasp.

In this rooftop setting the model on the left is wearing a blue flecked tweed Utility suit from fashion label Derata. The model on the right is wearing an emerald green woollen frock with matching jacket designed by Norman Hartnell. It cost 22 coupons.

This two-tone Atrima dress cost 7 coupons. In 1943 the clothes ration book had a total of 66 coupons in it.

Monsieur Jean, a master tailor at the house of designer Norman Hartnell, is pictured in the tailoring room cutting a model suit.

Here we see a scarlet and white spot-printed Utility rayon shirt dress with front-buttoning with accompanying white turban and white gloves. It was part of the Utility Clothing Scheme.

Here we see famous fashion designer Peter Russell sketching a new design in his London couture house.

Top 10 Girls' Baby Names [1]

1. Margaret — from *Margārīta*, the old Persian word meaning "Pearl"
2. Patricia — of Latin origin meaning "Noble Patrician"
3. Christine — of French and Latin origin meaning "Follower of Christ"
4. Mary — from the Latin *Stella Maris* – "Star of the Sea"
5. Jean — of Hebrew origin meaning "God is gracious"
6. Ann — of Hebrew origin meaning "God has favoured me"
7. Susan — of Hebrew origin meaning "Lily Rose"
8. Janet — of French origin meaning little Joan itself meaning "God's Gift"
9. Maureen — of Irish Gaelic origin meaning "Star of the Sea"
10. Barbara — of Latin origin meaning "Foreign Woman"

Top 10 Boys' Baby Names [2]

1. John — of Hebrew origin meaning "God has been gracious"
2. David — of Hebrew origin meaning "Beloved"
3. Michael — of Hebrew origin meaning "Who is like God?"
4. Peter — from the Greek *Petros* meaning "Rock"
5. Robert — from Old German meaning "Bright Fame"
6. Anthony — of Latin origin meaning "Priceless One"
7. Brian — of Celtic origin meaning "Strong, High and Noble"
8. Alan — from Old German meaning "Precious" or Gaelic meaning "Little Rock"
9. William — of Old German origin meaning "Resolute Protector"
10. James — from the Hebrew name *Jacob* meaning "Supplanter"

[1] [2] Data compiled by the Office for National Statistics 1944

Games, Toys and Pastimes

Games, toys and pastimes have always reflected the attitude and imagination of the culture that created them. During the War children played many different games that were handed down to them and invented a few of their own. Group games such as hopscotch, statues and hide and seek were popular as they required little or no equipment. Ball games were often played with improvised equipment for example a ball of rags for a football or a stick for a cricket bat. When real sports paraphernalia was available children were at the mercy of their owner who could call an end to the game at any time. Board games such as chess and checkers were played as were newer family games like Scrabble and Monopoly. Adults played bridge and gin rummy whilst young children contented themselves with snap and happy families. Meccano, a model construction system consisting of metal strips and nuts and bolts was popular with both children and adults. Whilst no new sets were produced, old ones were dusted off and hours of fun were had.

Building with Meccano

Celebrating Christmas in 1943

During World War II, Christmas in Britain was a subdued affair. Many families had loved ones fighting overseas, and the country was still experiencing the hardships of war, including rationing and bombing. However, the British people were resilient, and Christmas was still a time for celebration, even if it was a more modest one. One way that people tried to bring some cheer to the holiday season was by decorating their homes with what they had available. This might include handmade decorations such as paper chains, or even just a few sprigs of holly. Many people also put up Christmas trees, although these were often small and not as elaborately decorated as they might be in peacetime. Present giving was also more difficult during the war due to rationing. Many people made their own gifts, such as knitwear or baked goods, or exchanged small items that they had been able to obtain.

Others sent gifts to loved ones serving overseas. Christmas dinners were also more modest than they might have been in peacetime. The government had introduced rationing in 1940, which meant that people had to make do with less food. This included meat, which was in short supply. As a result, many Christmas dinners consisted of vegetables including potatoes, carrots, and Brussels sprouts. Despite the difficulties, the British people still found ways to enjoy the holiday season. There were carol singing events, pantomimes, and other festive gatherings. The BBC also broadcast special Christmas programmes, which many people listened to on

Father Christmas handing out toys to evacuees

the radio. In 1943, King George VI gave a radio address on Christmas Day, in which he spoke about the importance of unity and hope in difficult times. Overall, Christmas in Britain during 1943 was a time of both celebration and reflection. While the war was still ongoing, the people found ways to come together and enjoy the holiday season, despite the challenges they were facing. One popular holiday activity during this time was sending Christmas cards. Despite the difficulties of the war, people still found ways to communicate with each other and spread holiday cheer.

Christmas on-board HMS Malaya

Some people created their own cards, using whatever materials they had to hand. Others purchased cards from shops, although these were often more expensive and harder to come by due to the war. In addition to Christmas cards, many people also exchanged letters and packages with loved ones serving overseas. These often contained small gifts, such as food or other necessities, as well as letters and photos. These exchanges were a way for people to stay connected with their loved ones and let them know they were thinking of them during the holiday season. While the war had a significant impact on Christmas in Britain in 1943, it did not diminish the spirit of the holiday. The British people were known for their resilience and determination, and they found ways to come together and celebrate despite the challenges they were facing. So, Christmas in Britain during 1943 was a time of hope and celebration, even in the midst of a difficult and uncertain time.

In 1943 entertainment provided civilians with a form of escape from the privations of life in wartime. It was also important to those serving in the forces at home and overseas. There was no television as it was feared that the strong signal from London's Alexandra Palace could serve as a navigational aide for enemy aircraft. So in September 1939 following a cartoon, *Mickey's Gala Premier*, television services were halted. TV service resumed on 7th June 1946 and, after a brief opening ceremony the BBC, once again played the Mickey Mouse cartoon. By the start of the war only 20,000 households had TV sets as compared to 10 million radio licences. The cinema was also hugely popular, with films such as *Casablanca*, *The Gentle Sex* and *We'll Meet Again*, playing to packed houses. The films were often preceded by Pathé News, which gave audiences a heavily censored account of how the war was going.

Pathé News

Judy Garland

Theatres that had closed at the beginning of the war began to reopen and in March fans of classical music were thrilled to hear the first performance of Michael Tippet's *String Quartet No.2*. Not only were there no music charts in Britain in 1943, there was also no vinyl to make records. Production of Polyvinyl Chloride was used exclusively for the war effort. Instead people had to make do with music from the radio or pull out a record from their pre-war collection. Performers such as Flanagan and Allen and Vera Lynn were popular, as were Americans Bing Crosby and Judy Garland. British musical tastes were also widened by the influx of G.I.s who brought with them new musical genres such as Bebop, a fast-tempo form of jazz. The pub, that traditional hub of British life, provided homemade entertainment. Many a round was interrupted by a sing-a-long of *Knees Up Mother Brown* or *Roll Out the Barrel*.

Museums and art galleries in Britain's major cities had been emptied and their artefacts spirited away to the countryside for safekeeping. The National Gallery in London, though denuded of exhibits, was the scene of the most defiant of cultural events. The redoubtable pianist Myra Hess decided the show must go on and held a series of classical concerts at the gallery. If bombs fell too close, she simply moved the audience, lock stock and barrel, to the basement. She also helped to promote young performers such as Eiluned Davies who gave the premiere of Shostakovich's *Piano Sonata Op. 12* at the gallery on 31st May 1943.

The National Gallery with pianist Myra Hess (inset)

For Whom the Bell Tolls

Directed by Sam Wood
Starring Gary Cooper, Ingrid Bergman and Akim Tamiroff
Premiered 16th July 1943

The film is based on the 1940 novel of the same name by Ernest Hemingway, which tells the story of Robert Jordan, an American who fights with a Republican guerrilla unit during the Spanish Civil War. In the film, Jordan (played by Cooper) is a college professor and World War I veteran who volunteers to join the Republican forces in Spain. He is assigned to work with a group of guerrillas led by a man named Pablo (Tamiroff) and his wife, Pilar (Bergman). Jordan is tasked with blowing up a bridge to disrupt the movement of fascist forces, and he becomes romantically involved with a young woman named Maria (played by Katina Paxinou). As Jordan and the guerrillas prepare for the mission, they face challenges and dangers from both the enemy and their own internal conflicts. Jordan must confront his own personal demons and struggles with the ethical implications of his actions as he becomes more deeply involved in the war. *For Whom the Bell Tolls* was a critical and commercial success upon its release, and it received seven Academy Award nominations, including Best Picture and Best Actor for Cooper. The film is considered a classic of war cinema and is renowned for its performances, especially those of Cooper and Bergman, as well as its sweeping cinematography and emotionally powerful story.

Sherlock Holmes in Washington

Directed by Roy William Neill
Starring Basil Rathbone, Nigel Bruce and Marjorie Lord
Released on 30th April 1943

The film was produced by Universal Pictures and based on the story *The Adventure of the Silent Passenger* by Christopher Morley. In the film, Sherlock Holmes (Rathbone) is called to Washington, D.C. to investigate a missing secret document. He is accompanied by his trusty sidekick Dr. Watson (Bruce). The document, which contains information about the Allied invasion of Europe, has been stolen by Nazi spies and must be recovered before it falls into the wrong hands. Upon arriving in Washington, Holmes and Watson team up with a female FBI agent named Ann Brandon (Marjorie Lord) to track down the thieves. As they delve deeper into the case, they uncover a complex web of espionage and deceit, and must use all of their detective skills to solve the mystery. As with many of the Sherlock Holmes films, the plot is full of twists and turns, and the characters must use their wits and deduction skills to outmanoeuvre the villains. Despite being made during the height of World War II, the film manages to remain light and entertaining, with a good balance of action and humour. Although not one of the more enduring films in the Sherlock Holmes series, partly because it was not written by Conan Doyle, the movie enjoyed critical acclaim and box office success at the time.

Desert Victory

Directed by Roy Boulting
Script by Frank Launder and Sidney Gillat
Produced by the Film Units of the British Army and the RAF

Desert Victory is a 1943 British documentary film that chronicles the Allies' efforts in the North African Campaign of World War II, specifically the Battle of El Alamein. The film opens with a map of North Africa and a voice-over explaining the strategic importance of the region and the objectives of the Allies. It then cuts to footage of the desert landscape and the troops preparing for battle, intercut with interviews with soldiers and commanders on the ground. The film documents the various stages of the battle, including the initial British advance, the counter attack by the Germans and the final Allied victory. Much of the footage was film captured from the retreating Germans and this gives the movie an even-handed feel. One of the standout features of *Desert Victory* is the use of colour, which was relatively rare at the time. This added an extra level of realism to the film and allowed viewers to get a sense of the harsh desert conditions and the bravery of the soldiers on both sides. The film was a critical and commercial success upon its release and was widely praised for its authentic and unbiased portrayal of the conflict. It won several awards including a special Oscar and is still considered one of the best war documentaries of all time.

The Gentle Sex

Directed and Narrated by Leslie Howard
Starring Joan Greenwood, Joyce Howard and Rosamund John
Released 15th April 1943

This is a British propaganda film produced during World War II. It follows the lives of seven women who work in different roles supporting the war effort. The women are portrayed as strong and able, showing that women were capable of doing "men's work" and were an integral part of the push for victory. The film begins with the recruitment of the women and their training in various fields, including welding, driving, and nursing. As they begin their work, the women face challenges, obstacles and prejudice, but they persevere and prove themselves to be skilled and dedicated to their jobs. One of the women, Mary, becomes a welder and works on building ships for the navy. Another, Joan, trains as a nurse and goes to work in a military hospital. The film also follows a group of women who work as drivers, transporting troops and supplies. As the war continues, the women face dangers and personal loss, but they remain committed to their jobs and the war effort. The film ends with a victory parade in London, where the women march alongside their male counterparts, celebrating their contributions to the war. *The Gentle Sex* was intended to boost morale and encourage women to join the war effort, and it was widely praised for its positive portrayal of women. It is a testament to the strength and determination of women during a time of great crisis.

Casablanca

Directed by Michael Curtiz
Starring Humphrey Bogart, Ingrid Bergman and Paul Henreid
Went on general release in January 1943

Set against the backdrop of the war *Casablanca* was nominated for eight Academy Awards (Oscars) and won three in the categories Best Film, Best Director and Best Screenplay. The film stars screen icons Humphrey Bogart, in one of his more thoughtful roles, and Ingrid Bergman. Based on a stage play by Murray Burnett and Joan Alison, *Everyone Comes to Ricks*, it tells the story of a complicated love triangle with a heart-breaking ending. It ranks as one of the best movies of all time.

The cinematography captures the atmosphere of the North African city of Casablanca, while the fast-paced storyline fits in with the impending threat of conflict arriving on its doorstep. The piano man in the bar, Sam, played by Dooley Wilson, provides a moving soundtrack to the action. His rendition of the song *As Time Goes By*, perfectly bookends the relationship between the two main characters.

We'll Meet Again

Directed by Philip Brandon
Starring Vera Lynn, Geraldo, Patricia Roc and Ronald Ward
Released on 18th January 1943

"We'll Meet Again" is a 1943 British musical film starring Vera Lynn and is loosely based on her life as the 'Forces Sweetheart'. The film is set during the blitz in London and follows Peggy, a young dancer in a London music hall who discovers her singing talent during a bombing raid. Peggy and her best friend Frank, an aspiring songwriter, work on new songs together. An old school friend, Bruce, returns on leave from the Scots Guards and starts seeing Peggy, but confesses his love is for Peggy's friend, Ruth. Peggy reunites them and sings at their wedding. Peggy and Frank's demo gets played on BBC Radio and they both become successful musicians. Peggy makes a dedication to Bruce on a special radio broadcast, but he's missing in action. However, it turns out he was only wounded. The film ends with Peggy and Frank giving an open-air concert to several hundred RAF crew, singing "Sincerely Yours" and "We'll Meet Again". The film was a box office success and was well received by critics and audiences, it was praised for its realistic portrayal of life during the war and its strong performances by the cast.

ITMA

Ran from 12th July 1939 to 6th January 1949
Number of series: 12
Number of episodes: 305 plus 5 specials

Created by the writing team of Tommy Handley, the star of the show and Ted Kavanagh, *Its That Man Again*, ITMA, got off to the most inauspicious of starts. Set on a pirate radio station on a ship where Handley himself chose the programmes, it featured characters such as a mad Russian and Cilly, his "oh so silly" secretary. The show ran for four episodes and was not a great success.

When Hitler declared war on Britain, the BBC, scrabbling around for content, decided to award the comedy a run of 21 shows. A stalwart of British wartime radio was born. The setting for the new series was changed, as being set on a boat during a war was not credible. Instead Handley became Minister of Aggravation in the Ministry of Twerps. New characters were brought in including Funf, a German spy who satirised Nazi propaganda radio. The show was a success, perhaps not only because it lampooned the enemy, but possibly because it poked fun at the British government. This was too much for the BBC and by series three the writers moved the setting to a run down seaside resort called *Foaming at the Mouth*. The show ran for twelve series until January 1949.

Caribbean Voices

Ran from 1943 to Spring 1958
Presented by Henry Swanzy
Produced by Una Marson

Caribbean Voices was a BBC radio programme created with the aim of showcasing the work of Caribbean poets, writers and playwrights. The first episode of *Caribbean Voices* was broadcast on 11th June 1943 and featured a reading of the short story *The Dawn Comes Up Like Thunder* by the Guyanese writer Edgar Mittelholzer.

The programme was initially broadcast on the BBC's Empire Service, which was heard by listeners in Africa, the Caribbean, and other parts of the British Empire. The programme was later picked up by the BBC's Home Service, which made it available to listeners in the United Kingdom. The programme was presented by Henry Swanzy, a Jamaican-born broadcaster who had a deep passion for Caribbean literature and culture. Swanzy was responsible for selecting the works that were featured on the programme and for introducing each episode with a commentary. The programme was hugely popular and was credited with introducing many Caribbean writers to a wider audience. It featured some of the most well-known Caribbean authors such as George Lamming and Samuel Selvon (pictured) and was broadcast for over 15 years.

Desert Island Discs

From 27th January 1942 to present
Opening Theme: "By The Sleepy Lagoon" by Eric Coates
Number of episodes: Over 3200 and counting

Brainchild of freelance broadcaster Roy Plomley, this iconic BBC radio programme first took to the airways on 27th January, 1942. The idea came to him late one evening whilst in his pyjamas. He sent a pitch to BBC's Head of Popular Record Programmes, Leslie Perowne who liked the concept, perhaps because it offered an escapist fantasy in those troubled times. The initial recordings took place at the bomb damaged BBC studios in Maida Vale, West London. Plomley's first castaway was the popular exiled Austrian musician and comic actor, Vic Oliver, who also happened to be Winston Churchill's son-in-law. Oliver's first choice was Chopin's Étude No.12., performed by the virtuoso pianist, Alfred Cortot. On 7th May, Plomley himself became the castaway and Perowne the presenter. The programme ran throughout the war and was broadcast at home and to the troops abroad, finally coming off air in 1946, before returning to the Home Service in 1951. The original broadcasts offered the castaway no bible or complete works of Shakespeare, no book of their choice and certainly no luxury as it does today. Even in the fantasy world of a radio programme, in 1943, rationing prevailed.

The Kitchen Front

Ran from June 1940 to October 1943
Featuring Elsie and Doris Waters
Influenced by the Ministry of Food's Food Economy Campaign

One of the BBC's most important contributions to the war effort at home was through the radio programme *The Kitchen Front*. It combined information with humour and boosted morale during the dreary days of rationing. It featured ideas on how to make the most of ingredients and use up leftovers. *Feed the Beast* was an early amusing attempt to do so.

One day a week the programme was presented by the biggest female double act in British comedy, Elsie and Doris Waters. They were sisters who became popular in the 20s and 30s with their alter-egos Gert and Daisy. Together they made a large contribution to film and radio entertainment during the war, often talking about their fictional absent boyfriends/husbands Bert and Wally. More serious sections of the show saw "the Radio Doctor" Charles Hill, secretary of the British Medical Association, offer advice on health and well being. Ministers such as Lord Woolton would appear, taking advantage of the show's 7 million listenership, to broadcast public information.

Dooley Wilson

As Time Goes By

Performed by Dooley Wilson

From the film Casablanca (on general release January 1943)

Written by Herman Hupfeld

As Time Goes By was written in 1931 and sat in relative obscurity until the right context and the right singer came along. The tune provides much of the background music for the pivotal moments of the film Casablanca, and Wilson's rendition of the song coincides with the film's most heart-rending moment. Its words were instantly singable from the beginning "You must remember this, a kiss is just a kiss," to the final line "The world will always welcome lovers, as time goes by." It has been voted No.2 best movie song of all time by the American Film Institute only surpassed by *Over the Rainbow* from *The Wizard of Oz*.

Glenn Miller

That Old Black Magic

Performed by Glenn Miller and his Orchestra

Written by Harold Arlen (music) and Johnny Mercer (Lyrics)

Released in January 1943

The song, featuring vocals by Ray Eberle, was a hit for Miller, reaching #11 on the Billboard charts in 1943. The lyrics describe the irresistible and mysterious power of love, using the metaphor of "black magic" to convey the feeling of being under a spell. The song's popularity has endured through the decades and it is considered a classic of the Great American Songbook. Frank Sinatra recorded an upbeat arrangement of the song for his 1957 album *A Swingin' Affair!* contrasting with the more melancholy tone of the original. Sammy Davis Jr. recorded the song with a Latin influence for his 1962 album. Linda Ronstadt's contemplative interpretation featured on her 1976 album *Hasten Down the Wind*.

Lena Horne

Stormy Weather

Performed by Lena Horne

Released for the film Stormy Weather July 1943

Written by Harold Arlen and Ted Koehler

Horne's rendition of the song is known for its emotional delivery and powerful vocals. It showcases her range as a singer and her ability to convey the lyrics' message of heartbreak and longing. The song has been covered by many other artists over the years, but Horne's version is considered one of the most definitive. Throughout her career, Horne was also an important figure in the Civil Rights Movement and used her platform to promote racial equality. Despite facing discrimination and limited opportunities due to her race, she broke barriers in the entertainment industry and became one of the most successful African American performers of her time.

Bing Crosby

White Christmas

Sung by Bing Crosby
Written by Irving Berlin
Billboard No.1 single from January 2nd to January 9th 1943

The song paints a picture of Yuletide nostalgia and was written for the film *Holiday Inn*, where Crosby sings it from the point of view of a New Yorker living in sunny California yearning for snow. The original first line of the song reads "The sun is shining, the grass is green." Outside of the context of the film this made little sense and Berlin re-wrote the song to start with Crosby's deep mellifluous tones singing "I'm dreaming of a white Christmas." It soon became the Christmas song for this and many subsequent generations. It has gone on to become one of the most covered songs in history with versions by such disparate groups as St. Winifred's School Choir and the Irish punk band, Stiff Little Fingers.

Alice Faye

You'll Never Know (Just How Much I Love You)

Sung by Alice Faye
Released in 1943
Composed by Harry Warren with Lyrics by Mack Gordon

You'll Never Know was first heard as part of the 1943 film *Hello, Frisco, Hello* where it won the Academy Award for Best Original Song. Sung by Alice Faye she also performed it in the 1944 film *Four Jills in a Jeep*. However, the best loved version of the song was recorded by Vera Lynn. The lyrics perhaps express the longing and sadness of someone who has lost a loved one and the regret of not having realised how much they were loved while they were still alive. Vera Lynn's rendition was a huge success and helped to establish her as a popular wartime singer. The song has also been recorded by a plethora of stars including Ginger Rogers, Bing Crosby, Doris Day, Shirley Bassey. Barbara Streisand and Michael Bublé.

Noël Coward

Don't Let's Be Beastly to the Germans

Written and composed by Noël Coward
Released in 1943

Noël Coward, a British playwright, actor, and songwriter, enlisted with the British government at the start of the war. He was initially assigned to work in intelligence at Bletchley Park, but was later sent to Paris to work in the British propaganda bureau. He then embarked on a tour of the United States and Australia as a goodwill ambassador. Upon returning to London during the Blitz, he was unfazed by the threat of death from German bombs and even found the experience amusing. Prime Minister Winston Churchill felt Coward was wasting his time and ordered him to perform for troops in Europe, Africa, the Middle East, and Asia. *Don't Let's Be Beastly to the Germans* was popular when he performed it live but the humour didn't work over the wireless, leading the BBC to ban the song.

Dark is the Night

Mark Bernes

Performed by Mark Bernes

Released in October 1943

Composed by Nikita Bogoslovsky with Lyrics by Vladimir Agatov

Dark is the Night is a Soviet song associated with the Great Patriotic War (WWII). It was originally performed by Mark Bernes in the 1943 war film *Two Soldiers*. The song was composed by Nikita Bogoslovsky and lyrics by Vladimir Agatov specifically for the film. The song is a gentle, lyrical ballad that expresses a feeling of homesickness and devotion to one's loved ones. Despite official accusations of being a "Philistine" sentimental tune, it became a symbol of the war years for millions of Soviet people. It stands in contrast to the typical war songs which were field marching songs or civil patriotic ones. The song has since been covered by Russian poet and musician Bulat Okudzhava, and the Russian singer Lev Leshchenko.

Lili Marlene

Marlene Dietrich

Performed by Marlene Dietrich

First broadcast on Soldatensender Calais (Soldiers' Radio) in 1943

Written by Hans Leip (as a poem), Music by Norbert Schultze

Soldatensender Calais was a British "black" propaganda radio station operated by the Political Warfare Executive. It pretended to be a radio station of the German military network with the aim of creating friction between the Axis forces to undermine their morale. For the station the American OSS (precursor to the CIA) created high quality programming recruiting Hollywood talent including Marlene Dietrich and Bing Crosby. Dietrich's version of *Lili Marlene* which was first recorded in 1939 by Lale Andersen had some lyrics altered by the OSS team to align with the Allies' goals. It became a hit with Axis soldiers and was played at the end of every broadcast. It helped undermine their belief in Nazi propaganda.

Let's Get Lost

Mary Martin

Performed by Mary Martin

Released in January 1943

Composed by Jimmy McHugh with Lyrics by Frank Loesser

The actress Mary Martin performed this song in the 1943 film *Happy Go Lucky*. The song has a slow and romantic feel, with lyrics that express a desire to escape reality and get lost in love. It was written when the war as at it height and reflects the general feeling of longing and uncertainty that many people experienced during that time. The song's lyrics invite the listener to forget about their troubles and lose themselves in the moment, to focus on love and romance rather than the war and its aftermath. It is often considered a classic of the jazz genre and has been a staple of jazz playlists to this day. It has been covered by a variety of artists as diverse as Chet Baker, Van Morrison and Johnny Nash.

Live Jazz in London

Glenn Miller

Jazz was first heard at 100 Oxford Street, London during the winter of 1942/43 when British jazz drummer Victor Feldman's father hired the venue to showcase the talents of his jazz playing sons and their band. The concerts at Mack's restaurant, as it was then known, soon became a weekly occurrence.

News of the venue spread quickly leading to American servicemen and locals filling the club. Many of the American G.I's were talented performers in their own right and several impromptu performances took place. It was also a mighty relief to many American's that there was no racial segregation in Britain like there was at home meaning people were able to mix freely.

An early visitor to the club was legendary American bandleader Glenn Miller who performed several sets with his band. Quite often, as people partied through the night, bombs would fall, but they carried on regardless safe in the knowledge that the club's basement location made it a very effective shelter. Though the club has gone through many name changes throughout the decades, it is still running as the 100 Club today.

The Promenade Concerts

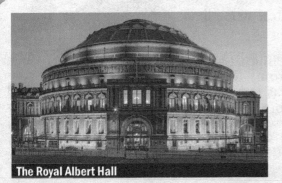

The Royal Albert Hall

The 1943 Proms were held during a time of great uncertainty and hardship for the British people. Despite the difficult circumstances, the concerts were well-attended and featured a wide variety of music from both classical and contemporary composers. The Proms featured a total of 66 concerts, which were held at the Royal Albert Hall. The concerts were organised by the BBC and were intended to provide a source of entertainment and cultural enrichment for the British public during the war. The concerts featured a mix of orchestral, choral, and solo performances, with many of the performances being broadcast on the BBC radio. The concerts featured a number of notable performers, including Sir Adrian Boult, who conducted several of the Proms, and pianist Myra Hess, who gave a series of solo performances.

The concerts also featured works by a number of contemporary composers, such as Benjamin Britten, Ralph Vaughan Williams, and William Walton. Many of the concert performances were dedicated to the war effort, with works such as Elgar's *Nimrod* and *Land of Hope and Glory* and Parry's *Jerusalem* being performed as patriotic tributes to the country and its soldiers.

The Nobel Prize in Literature was not awarded in 1943. The main literature prizes were handed out in America. The Pulitzer prize for best novel went to Upton Sinclair for *Dragon's Teeth*, a story of a socialist grandson of an American arms manufacturer. Time Magazine wrote "Few works of fiction are more fun to read; fewer still make history half as clear, or as human". The prize in poetry was awarded to Robert Frost for his collection *A Witness Tree*. Thornton Wilder scooped the best drama award for *The Skin of our Teeth*, a modern day working of parts of the Old Testament. The best history prize went to Ester Forbes for *Paul Revere and the World He Lived In*, in which she paints a memorable portrait of American colonial history. In Britain George Orwell resigned from his position at the BBC to become editor of the left-wing London newspaper *Tribune*. H.G. Wells

Upton Sinclair

released *Crux Ansata*, a visceral attack on the Catholic Church and Graham Greene wrote a tense wartime thriller *Ministry of Fear*, a tale of Nazi espionage set in the London of the Blitz. In children's literature Enid Blyton produced two books, *The Mystery of the Burnt Cottage* and *The Faraway Tree*. In December, the country lost its greatest children's writer and illustrator, Beatrix Potter, who died aged 77.

T.S. Eliot

George Orwell

In December poet Philip Larkin, having graduated from Oxford, obtained his first post as librarian in Wellington, Shropshire. His most poignant poem of the year was *A Stone Church Damaged by a Bomb*. T.S Eliot saw the publication of his *Four Quartets*, which brought together his poems of 1940-42. After this, he fell out of love with poetry. In art, in August 1943 Leonardo Da Vinci's *The Last Supper* came close to obliteration when an Allied heavy bombardment hit the Santa Maria delle Grazie church in Milan. The painting is a mural on its wall. Miraculously, as the smoke and dust cleared the great work of art was revealed to be relatively unscathed. In Britain L.S. Lowry served as a fire watcher in Manchester. He was stationed on city-centre rooftops and recalled being the "first on the scene in the morning to sketch the blitzed buildings before the smoke and grime cleared".

Da Vinci's The Last Supper mural was nearly destroyed

The Saint Steps In

Author: Leslie Charteris   First British Edition Published: 1943

Simon Templar, also known as "The Saint", after his initials ST, was a gentleman thief and adventurer who travelled the world getting involved in all sorts of exciting and dangerous escapades. This novel, written towards the end of the war, is a typical *Saint* plot. A beautiful woman is in danger because of her innocent involvement in a criminal scheme. All this is set against the background of one of the most important industries for the war effort, rubber production. In many ways, *The Saint Steps In* could be considered a paradigm for *Saint* novels. It is an exciting thriller and also an uncompromising attack on the elements of society that Charteris despised. In this case these were Nazis, fifth columnists, profiteers and those who, through stupidity, allowed these people to operate. In 1962 *The Saint* was brought to television screens, with Roger Moore playing the debonair Simon Templar.

Arrival and Departure

Author: Arthur Koestler   Published: December 1943

It is spring 1941: Peter Slavek has escaped from his country, where the Movement has surrendered to an oppressive dictatorship. A student-hero who has survived interrogation by torture, Peter arrives in Neutralia (believed to be Portugal, based on the author's own experience fighting in the Spanish Civil War), a tense clearing-house for refugees en-route for uneasy peace or total war. Among them is Odette, a beautiful young widow; Bernard, a bi-sexual fascist proselytiser; and the psychologist Dr. Sonia Bolgar, who gives Peter the run of her flat in return for the run of his mind. Koestler's nightmare-allegory hinges on the dilemma of the revolutionary who realises that power can corrupt not only its wielders, but also its victims. *Arrival and Departure* is Koestler's most autobiographical work and although under 200 pages long is an intense and gripping read, detailing the everyday struggles of those drawn into the conflict.

The Lady in the Lake

Author: Raymond Chandler   Publication Date: 1943

In this novel, set in Los Angeles, Philip Marlowe is hired by a woman named Crystal Kingsley to find her missing husband, Derace Kingsley. His investigation leads him on a journey through the seedy underbelly of Los Angeles, where he encounters a cast of shady characters and uncovers a web of deceit and corruption. As Marlowe delves deeper into the case, he uses his wit and intelligence to outwit those who seek to harm him. Along the way, he also grapples with his own feelings of loneliness and isolation, and wonders if he will ever find true love. *The Lady in the Lake* is considered a classic of the hardboiled detective genre and is highly praised for its complex plot, vivid characterisations and crisp, noirish prose. The book was written shortly after the attack on Pearl Harbour and makes several references to America's recent involvement in World War II. It was adapted for cinema in 1947 starring Robert Montgomery and Audrey Totter.

A Tree Grows in Brooklyn
Author: Betty Smith   First Published: 8th August 1943

The beloved American classic about a young girl's coming-of-age at the turn of the 20th century, Betty Smith's *A Tree Grows in Brooklyn* is a poignant and moving tale filled with compassion and cruelty, laughter and heartache, crowded with life and people and incident. The story of a young, sensitive, and idealistic Francie Nolan and her bittersweet formative years in the slums of Williamsburg has enchanted and inspired millions of readers for more than eighty years. By turns overwhelming, sublime, heartbreaking and uplifting, the daily experiences of the unforgettable Nolans are raw with honesty and tenderly threaded with family connectedness in a work of literary art that brilliantly captures a unique time and place, as well as incredibly rich moments of universal experience. It tells a story of hardship and redemption and is an American classic.

The Ship
Author: C.S. Forester   First Published: 1943

The book is a good account of a Royal Navy ship in a single engagement during WWII. This book was written in an attempt to lift the morale of the British at home and around the world, but it is more than just simple propaganda. The author explains both the technology and the tactics of a cruiser engaging a superior force by getting into the heads of officers and ratings; all with many different roles to play in running the ship during combat and at normal times. This cast of characters is not all noble, but each is an interesting, surprisingly frank character combined with an account of what they are doing as a part of their normal job. This book is dedicated to the men and ship's company of HMS Penelope, a fast cruiser which was one of the ships responsible for supplying Malta. The ship in the novel, HMS Artemis, is fictional as are all her company but it reads as if it is a true story.

Hungry Hill
Author: Daphne du Maurier   First Published: 1943

Hungry Hill is an historical novel telling the story of several generations of the Brodrick family in Ireland spanning a tumultuous century from 1820 to 1920. It starts out with the story of "Copper" John Brodrick who starts a copper mine on Hungry Hill outside of the Brodrick estate at Castle Clonmere. Brodrick opens the mine in hope of making life better for his family and the people of the town. However it is frowned upon by most of the community of Doonhaven, especially by the family that formerly owned the land, the Donovans. Old man Donovan tells "Copper" John that "your mine will be in ruins and your home destroyed and your children forgotten, but this hill will be standing still to confound you." So the Donovan curse passes through the generations of Brodricks with tragedy awaiting most of the successors to the copper fortune. Overall, this book has a feeling of melancholia throughout with impending doom coming to the family.

The Gremlins
Author: Roald Dahl   First Published: 1943

The Gremlins is a short story by Roald Dahl and was his first published work. It is about a group of mischievous creatures that cause problems for pilots during World War II. Drawing heavily on the author's own wartime experience, the story begins with a young pilot named Gus who is on a bombing mission over Germany. Gus and his fellow pilots are plagued by a series of mishaps and mechanical failures, which they attribute to gremlins - mythical creatures that are said to cause mischief on planes. Gus becomes obsessed with catching a gremlin and sets a trap. When he finally succeeds in catching one, he is shocked to find that it is a small, intelligent creature with a British accent. The gremlin reveals that it and its fellow gremlins are actually trying to help the pilots by sabotaging their planes to prevent them from being shot down by the enemy. The story ends with Gus releasing the gremlin and promising to keep its existence a secret.

Mary Poppins Opens The Door
Author: P.L. Travers   First Published: 1943

This book is a British children's fantasy novel by the Australian-British writer P.L. Travers, the third book and last novel in the Mary Poppins series that features the magical English nanny. She arrives in the wake of the last fireworks display by the Banks family. The children Michael, Jane, the twins, and Annabel plead with her to stay. Mrs. Banks has Mary and the children find a piano tuner, who happens to be Mary's cousin, Mr. Twigley. When Mary and the children visit, Mr. Twigley tries to unburden himself of seven wishes given to him when he was born. The book is full of magic and charm and the finale sees several characters from the two previous books gather to wish Mary goodbye. It ends when Mr. Banks sees a shooting star, and they all wish upon it, the children faintly make out Mary Poppins. They wave and she waves back to them. "Mary Poppins herself had flown away, but the gifts she had brought would remain for always."

The Picts and The Martyrs (part of the Swallows and Amazons series)
Author: Arthur Ransome   First Published: 1943

Dick and Dorothea are staying with Nancy and Peggy, the Amazons, at Beckfoot. But Great Aunt comes to visit and she must not know the "Ds" are staying so they go to camp in an old hut in the woods, learning to tickle trout and to skin and cook a rabbit. Meanwhile Timothy is staying in Captain Flint's houseboat and needs Dick to burgle Beckfoot to get important chemicals. In many ways this is one of Ransome's best books. The story-telling is superb and he spins a classic adventure yarn from a simple summer holiday. As always the characters are perfect, with the portrayal of Nancy being at its best. You even empathise with the Great Aunt before the end. One of the wonderful things about Ransome is that he never talked down to his audience, explaining things in grown-up terms. For example: "I'll just hoist the sail for you. You take the halliard through the ring in the bows and it acts as a forestay."

Celeste Holm starred

Oklahoma!

Written by Richard Rodgers and Oscar Hammerstein II
Starring Betty Garde, Celeste Holm, Alfred Drake and Joan Roberts
Opened at the St. James Theatre, New York on 31st March 1943

When *Oklahoma!* first premiered on Broadway, much was at stake for the creators and the production team. Many were sceptical that an interesting musical could be crafted from a moderately successful homespun play about ranchers and farmers in the middle of America. Nevertheless, on a dank Wednesday night in March at the St. James Theatre, the first collaboration of Richard Rodgers and Oscar Hammerstein II played its opening night performance, and the reaction was extraordinary. The next morning, rave reviews for *Oklahoma!* poured in, and the box office was frenzied with theatregoers eager to claim their ticket to see the new musical that critics were calling "a striking piece of theatrical Americana." Choreographer Agnes de Mille's groundbreaking contribution was noted and applauded. Starring Betty Garde, Celeste Holm, Alfred Drake, Joan Roberts, and Howard da Silva, the original Broadway production of *Oklahoma!* went on to play a staggering 2,212 performances, running for nearly five years and holding the record for the longest-running Broadway musical for 15 years, until it was beaten by *My Fair Lady*. In its first year, *Oklahoma!* received a special Pulitzer Prize, and the original production launched an international tour that stopped in 361 cities around the world for nearly ten years. Songs such as *Oh What a Beautiful Mornin'* and *Kansas City* soon became firm favourites. A film version starring Gordon MacRae and Gloria Grahame was released in 1965.

The cast of US soldiers

This Is The Army

Music and Lyrics by Irving Berlin
Starring a cast of US soldiers
Opened in London on 10th November 1943

This Is The Army is an American musical revue that was produced by the U.S. army originally premiering on Broadway in 1942. The show was designed to boost morale with proceeds going to the Army Emergency Relief Fund. In 1941 Irving Berlin was on tour in America and visited Camp Upton in Yaphank, New York where he served as a Sergeant in World War I. Whilst there he suggested to the commanding officers that he restage his 1917 army play *Yip Yip Yaphank*. Berlin was granted permission to include African Americans in his play, despite the Army's insistence on racial segregation. This was a departure from the restrictions imposed on him for his previous production. The show opened on Broadway for an anticipated 4-week run but was so successful that it ran for 12 weeks. It was then decided to take the show on tour with initial dates within the United States. The cast arrived in the United Kingdom late in 1943 for a 17-night run at the London Palladium followed by the Glasgow Empire. Money raised from these performances went to British service charities. There was also a stipulation that "the soldiers of our Allies, as well as all American enlisted men, should see this Army show free of cost." The show raised over $2 million in total.

Blithe Spirit

Written by Noël Coward
Premiered on the 16th June 1941 at the Manchester Opera House
Resident throughout 1943 at the Duchess Theatre in the West End

Noël Coward

The comic play, described by Coward as a comedic farce in three acts, sees socialite and novelist Charles Condomine inviting a medium, Madame Arcati, to his home to conduct a séance for research on his next book. However, the plan goes awry when Charles's deceased first wife, Elvira, begins to haunt him and disrupt his current marriage to his second wife, Ruth, who cannot perceive the ghost. The title of the play is taken from Shelley's poem *To A Skylark* which includes the line *"Hail to thee, blithe spirit! Bird thou never wert,"* The idea originated after Coward's London office and apartment were destroyed during the Blitz; to escape London he took a brief holiday with actress Joyce Carey in Portmeirion in Wales. Coward recalled: "We sat on the beach with our backs against the sea wall and discussed my idea for a comedy play about ghosts for several hours." He then worked relentlessly for six days until the play was finished claiming "...with disdaining archness and false modesty, I will admit that I knew it was witty, I knew it was well constructed, and I also knew that it would be a success." He was right. It has been staged ever since including a recent screen adaptation in the 2020 film starring Dan Stevens and Dame Judi Dench.

Laurence Olivier

He may have been one of the most talented actors of his generation, a success both on stage and screen, but Olivier was a woeful military aviator. Both planes and pilots were precious commodities, yet in his short career in the Royal Navy's Fleet Air Arm, Olivier wrote off at least three aircraft. While he did provide the service with some magnificent photo opportunities, some argued that they came at too high a price. He may not have been a talented pilot but there was no doubting his courage. The dated design of many of the planes with open cockpits, made even training fraught with danger. Once rumours of Olivier requisitioning a plane to take his wife Vivien Leigh to lunch began to swirl, the authorities had had enough. After several years of military service and rising to the rank of Lieutenant, Whitehall decided that Olivier's much more obvious acting talent would better serve the war effort. The Ministry of Information asked him to take on the film role of *Henry V* which he also produced and directed. Olivier was proud of his achievements in the air and listed flying as one of his hobbies in his Who's Who entry.

Laurence Olivier

Revudeville

Created by Laura Henderson and Vivian Van Damm
The Windmill Theatre, Soho, London
'Never closed, Never clothed'

The Windmill Theatre

In 1930 Laura Henderson bought a cinema in Great Windmill Street, London and modelled it into a 320-seat two tier theatre. The Windmill Theatre was born. She hired a manager, Vivian Van Damm, who developed a show called Revudeville, a mixture of French Burlesque and American Vaudeville. Before the war the theatre's raunchy shows attracted a certain type of gentleman in a certain type of Mackintosh coat. The shows were performed under the watchful eye of The Lord Chamberlain's Office and nudes had to stand stock still. It is true to say that the war made the Windmill. London's Theatreland all but closed, but the Windmill didn't.

Henderson hit upon the idea of offering a number of free tickets to soldiers. The atmosphere changed overnight. British soldiers mingled with the Free French Army and later American G.I.'s, all hoping to catch a glimpse of something naughty. If a seat became available near the front, the men would often fight in order to secure it. After the war Soho gradually became more seedy, the Windmill's shows seemed tame by comparison, and its popularity declined. It will however be remembered as the "Theatre that never closed."

The Lisbon Story

Written by Harold Purcell, Music by Harry Parr-Davies
Premiered on 31st May 1943
at The Imperial Theatre, Brighton then The London Hippodrome

Noele Gordon
credit: The Noele Gordon Archive

The Lisbon Story is a 1943 British musical. The story is a wartime espionage thriller set in the cities of Lisbon and Paris during the summer of 1942. The story revolves around a Parisian singing star, Gabrielle Girard, and British Foreign Office agent David Warren. They meet in Lisbon, a neutral city in WWII, where David and his co-agent are caring for Lisette Sargon. Her scientist father is captured by Nazis, but Gabrielle helps secure his release and reunite him with Lisette. However, a Nazi representative threatens to reveal their secrets unless Gabrielle becomes his mistress. David and Mike attempt to smuggle them to London, using a patriotic musical performance as a diversion. The story ends with gunfire and bombs as they make their escape. Amongst the cast was a young Noele Gordon who would go on to reach iconic status as Meg Mortimer in the soap opera *Crossroads*. The show was a big hit and ran for over a year at the London Hippodrome. In 1946 the musical was adapted as a film with several actors reprising their roles from the stage. The song, *Pedro the Fisherman*, became a hit and was subsequently recorded by many artists including Gracie Fields and Julie Andrews.

Going to Work by L.S. Lowry

Laurence Stephen Lowry was a British painter known for his urban landscapes and industrial scenes. He was born in 1887 in Stretford, Lancashire, and worked as a clerk while pursuing his passion for painting in his spare time. Lowry's work often depicted the life and people of the industrial towns in the north of England, such as Manchester and Salford, and he is considered one of the most important artists of the 20th century. In 1943 *Going to Work* was commissioned by the War Artists Advisory Committee as part of an initiative to create a visual record of Britain during World War II. It depicts crowds of workers walking into the Mather & Platt engineering equipment factory in Manchester, England. The painting is considered a typical example of Lowry's industrial scenes, with "matchstalk" figures and an evocation of industrial haze in the background. Lowry was paid 25 guineas for the commission and it was completed in three months. It is now on public display in the Imperial War Museum North, alongside works by other artists such as Flora Lion and Anna Airy. Despite achieving commercial success during his lifetime, Lowry remained humble and dedicated to his craft until his death in 1976. In 1978, Lowry's work was evocatively captured in the number one song, *Matchstalk Men and Matchstalk Cats and Dogs,* by folk duo Brian and Michael.

Trafalgar Square by Piet Mondrian

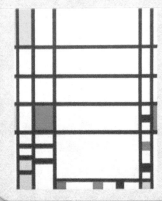

Pieter Cornelis Mondrian was a Dutch painter and art theorist who is considered one of the greatest artists of the 20th century. His work influenced not only the course of abstract painting and numerous major styles and art movements but also fields outside the domain of painting, such as design, architecture and fashion. *Trafalgar Square* was a painting that Mondrian started in 1939 whilst living in London having left Paris a year earlier over fears of a German invasion. In 1940 Mondrian then moved to America. Overall he worked on the painting for 4 years until 1943 when he applied the finishing touches whilst living in New York. Interestingly Mondrian was not always an abstract artist; in the first part of his career he painted in the classical impressionist style.

Sidney Keyes | War Poet

Sidney Keyes

Keyes started his military training in the Spring of 1942, but the dreamy poet was ill-suited to life in the army, much to the despair of his training officers. However, he was commissioned into The Queen's Old Royal West Kents, his father's old regiment, in October 1942. In the few months before being posted overseas he spent his leave with his lover Renée-Jane Scott, which inspired him to write his second poetry collection *The Cruel Solstice*. In March 1943 his unit was shipped out to fight in the North African theatre. His letters and a later published notebook evidenced a calm acceptance of his fate. His men respected him for his courage and steadfastness, even though he only lasted less than three weeks. He died in the Tunisian Mountains near Sidi Abdulla during an attack on a fortified hill at dusk on 29th April. He was last sighted fighting back-to-back with a comrade as they tried to stave off a German counter-attack. There is mystery about the precise circumstances of his death and burial that may never be fully resolved. *The Collected Poems of Sidney Keyes*, edited by Michael Meyer, was published in 1944 to much contemporary praise. To the critic Geoffrey Hill, Keyes was a 'Gothic pastoralist', to another, Owen Lowery, he was 'an exiled lover in harmony with nature and at odds with the violence of his time'. What is clear is that he gave us some fine poems and this work promised greater things that would never come to fruition. Keyes' own image of himself was that of a candle flame rising up and burning more brightly just as it was on the point of extinction. One of his last poems addressed the futility of war.

War Poet

Written by Sidney Keyes

I am the man who looked for peace and found
My own eyes barbed.
I am the man who groped for words and found
An arrow in my hand.
I am the builder whose firm walls surround
A slipping land.
When I grow sick or mad
Mock me not nor chain me:
When I reach for the wind
Cast me not down:
Though my face is a burnt book
And a wasted town.

Elva Blacker - War Artist

Painter Elva Blacker in WAAF uniform

Few people documented the war better than Elva Blacker. Whilst most did it with a pen or a film camera, Elva, who trained at Slade School of Fine Art, did it with pencils, watercolours and inks. Having served as a driver for the Blood Transfusion Service, in 1942 she joined up to the Women's Auxiliary Air Force. It was here she combined her dedication to service with her passion for art.

Military life is punctuated with periods of calm when participants have to recharge and stave off boredom. Through her portraiture Elva provided therapy for both the artist and the sitter. She would relax the subject by engaging in conversation and this shines through in the intimacy of her work. Her value as a war artist and the pleasure others derived from it gave her free reign to record sick quarters, crew rooms and the officers' mess. As a result she produced an unrivalled record of everyday life in RAF stations. In 1943 she exhibited some of her single and group portraits at the National Portrait Gallery.

Jackson Pollock - The Father of Abstract Expressionism

Jackson Pollock (aged 16)

Jackson Pollock was an American painter and a major figure in the abstract expressionist movement known for his technique of pouring or splattering paint onto the canvas. His work was heavily influenced by the work of the Surrealists and the indigenous art of the American West. His technique of "action painting," in which he would drip or pour paint onto a horizontal canvas, was a way for him to tap into the unconscious mind and create unique and dynamic compositions. In 1943, Jackson Pollock had his first solo exhibition at the Guggenheim Gallery in New York City. The exhibition was curated by Peggy Guggenheim, who had become a patron of Pollock's work. The show featured around fifteen works, including his iconic drip paintings. The exhibition catalogue described Pollock's talent as "volcanic. It has fire. It is unpredictable. It is undisciplined. It spills out of itself in a mineral prodigality, not yet crystallised." The exhibition received mixed reviews, but it was a pivotal moment in his career, helping to establish Pollock as a major figure in the Abstract Expressionist movement. Pollock was reclusive and had a volatile personality. He struggled with alcoholism throughout his life. He died aged just 44 from an alcohol-related single-car collision in which he was driving.

The Kidney Dialysis Machine

The Kolff artificial drum kidney

Kidney dialysis is a medical treatment that is used to remove waste and excess fluid from the blood when the kidneys are unable to function properly. Dialysis was first used in 1943 by Dutch physician Willem Johan Kolff, who developed the first artificial kidney machine, called the "artificial kidney." Kolff's machine used a rotating drum filled with cellulose material to filter the blood. Initial trials were unsuccessful until, in 1945, a 67-year-old comatose woman regained consciousness after 11 hours of dialysis. She lived for a further 7 years. It was the first successful treatment for a patient with acute renal failure. In the 1950s and 1960s, dialysis technology continued to improve, and the use of dialysis became more widespread. The first successful use of hemodialysis, which uses a semipermeable membrane to filter the blood, was performed in 1960. In the following decades, advances in dialysis technology allowed for longer and more frequent treatments, and the development of peritoneal dialysis, which uses the lining of the abdominal cavity to filter the blood, expanded treatment options for patients with chronic renal failure. Despite significant advancements in dialysis technology, the search for a cure for kidney disease continues, with researchers working to develop more effective and less invasive treatments.

The First Airborne, Ground Scanning Radar

H2S black radomes visible on the noses of these Avro Vulcan bombers pictured in 1957

H2S radar was the first airborne, ground scanning radar system developed for the Royal Air Force's Bomber Command during World War II. It went into service in 1943 and was used to detect objects on the ground, such as ships and buildings, from an aircraft. Prior to the development of H2S radar, aircraft relied on visual sightings to locate targets, which was difficult at night or in poor weather conditions. H2S radar allowed aircraft to locate targets even in adverse conditions, greatly improving their ability to carry out bombing missions. The first operational use of H2S radar was by the Royal Air Force in February 1943. It was used extensively during the war and proved to be a valuable tool for the Allies. After the war, H2S radar technology was further developed and is still in use today in various forms. A tragic footnote to the story is that the chief designer of the system, the prolific Alan Blumlein, was killed along with two colleagues when their test flight crashed in June 1942.

The Aqua Lung

Jacques-Yves Cousteau

The Aqua Lung, also known as the scuba diving regulator, was invented by French naval officer and explorer Jacques Cousteau and engineer Émile Gagnan in 1943. The Aqua Lung allowed divers to breathe underwater for extended periods of time, greatly expanding the possibilities for underwater exploration and research. Prior to its invention, divers were limited to using breathing tubes or bulky, heavy diving suits that allowed for only short periods of time underwater. Cousteau and Gagnan's invention was based on the principle of using compressed air tanks to supply air to the diver, who could then breathe normally through a regulator. The Aqua Lung was an immediate success, and Cousteau and Gagnan founded the company La Spirotechnique in 1946 to manufacture and sell the device. The Aqua Lung was not only a practical tool for divers, but it also allowed for the exploration of new, previously inaccessible areas of the ocean. Cousteau and Gagnan's invention revolutionised the field of underwater exploration and paved the way for the development of modern scuba diving equipment. Today, the Aqua Lung is used by millions of recreational and professional divers around the world.

The Slinky

The Slinky was created by accident

In 1943 a naval mechanical engineer was searching for a way to keep sensitive equipment on ships from being damaged during rough seas by suspending them using torsion springs. During his experiments he accidentally knocked a spring off a shelf and was surprised to see it "walk" down a set of steps. The engineer was Richard James and it was this moment that gave him the idea to create the Slinky as a toy for children. He and his wife Betty initially struggled to find a manufacturer for their new toy, but eventually they were able to produce it in small quantities. The slinky was first sold at Gimbels department store in Philadelphia in 1945, and it was an instant success. The Jameses were able to keep up with the demand for their toy by setting up their own factory, and the slinky quickly became a cultural phenomenon. In the decades since its invention, the slinky has remained a popular toy, with over 300 million units sold worldwide. It has been featured in numerous television shows and movies including Disney Pixar's *Toy Story* that features the Slinky dog character. The Slinky was inducted into the US National Toy Hall of Fame in 2000. Despite its simple design, the slinky continues to delight and fascinate people of all ages.

The Colossus Computer

Operating the Colossus in 1943

The Colossus computer was the world's first programmable electronic digital computer, developed by British codebreakers during World War II to help decipher German messages encrypted with the Lorenz cipher. It was operational in December 1943 at Bletchley Park, the British codebreaking headquarters. The Colossus was designed and built by a team led by British engineer Tommy Flowers, and was a massive machine that used vacuum tubes and was able to perform a wide range of complex calculations at high speeds. The Colossus helped the British codebreakers make significant progress in deciphering the Lorenz messages, which contained valuable military intelligence. After the war, the Colossus computers were dismantled and destroyed. The Colossus is an important milestone in the history of computing, and paved the way for the development of modern computers. The work of the codebreakers at Bletchley Park, and the development of the Colossus, is now widely recognised as having played a crucial role in the Allied victory in World War II. The technology used in the Colossus was revolutionary for its time, and its development was a significant step forward in the field of computing.

Project Y

Bomb assembly at Los Alamos

Project Y, also known as the Los Alamos Laboratory, was a research and development facility in New Mexico that played a key role in the development of the first atomic bombs during World War II. The project was part of the larger Manhattan Project, which was a secret U.S. government effort to develop nuclear weapons during the war. The laboratory was established in 1943 on the site of a boys' school in Los Alamos, New Mexico, and was initially directed by physicist J. Robert Oppenheimer. The goal of Project Y was to design and build the world's first atomic bombs. The laboratory was a high-security facility, and the work that took place there was highly secretive. In 1945, the laboratory successfully developed and tested the first atomic bombs, which were dropped on the Japanese cities of Hiroshima and Nagasaki later that year. After the war, the Los Alamos Laboratory continued to operate as a research facility and played a key role in the development of the hydrogen bomb in the 1950s. Today, the laboratory is still in operation and is one of the U.S. government's premier research and development facilities for national security-related science and technology.

The Discovery of Streptomycin

Making a streptomycin assay

Streptomycin is an antibiotic drug that was discovered in 1943 by Selman Waksman and his graduate student Albert Schatz. They found the drug in a soil sample from the University of California, Berkeley, where Waksman was studying soil microorganisms. The drug was isolated from the bacterium Streptomyces griseus and was named streptomycin for the bacteria's genus name. In 1944, streptomycin was tested on mice infected with the bacteria that causes tuberculosis and was found to be effective in killing the bacteria. In the following years, streptomycin was used to successfully treat a number of bacterial infections, including pneumonia, and meningitis. In the 1950s, streptomycin became the first generally prescribed antibiotic to be used in the treatment of tuberculosis, which was a major public health problem at the time. However, its widespread use has led to the emergence of antibiotic-resistant strains of bacteria. Despite this, streptomycin remains an important drug in the treatment of bacterial infections and is often used in combination with other antibiotics to increase its effectiveness.

The Drug That Treated Churchill

Winston Churchill pictured in 1943

Sulfapyridine is a sulfa drug that was developed in the 1930s as a treatment for bacterial infections. It was discovered by Swiss chemist Paul F. May and German chemist Alfred Faust, who were working for the pharmaceutical company Bayer at the time. It was first synthesised in 1935 and was found to be effective in treating bacterial infections of the skin and respiratory tract. In 1943, British Prime Minister Winston Churchill was suffering from pneumonia, and was treated with sulfapyridine as part of his recovery. Churchill's doctors credited the drug with helping him to recover from the illness, and it was widely reported in the press at the time. Sulfapyridine was widely prescribed in the 1940s and 1950s. However, its use declined in the 1960s due to the discovery of more effective antibiotics, such as penicillin. Today, sulfapyridine is still used in the treatment of bacterial infections, but it is generally reserved for cases where other antibiotics are not effective. It is also used in the treatment of inflammatory bowel disease, and is often used with other drugs to maximise its effectiveness.

United Kingdom

In 1943, British military innovation focused on several key areas, including aircraft technology, naval warfare, and infantry tactics.

One major innovation in aircraft technology was the development of the jet engine. The British had been working on jet technology since the 1930s, and in 1943 they were able to test fly what would become the first operational military jet fighter, the Gloster Meteor. Although it was prone to stability issues at high speeds due to poor aerodynamics, it was still an important milestone in aviation history. The Meteors were first deployed at RAF Manston in 1944 briefed to seek out and destroy incoming German V-1 rockets.

A pair of F.3 Gloster Meteors patrolling the skies

An X-class midget submarine in action

In naval warfare, the British introduced several new technologies and tactics. One important innovation was the use of midget submarines; small, highly manoeuvrable submarines that could be used for a variety of tasks, including laying mines and conducting covert operations. The British also developed new types of naval mines, including magnetic mines that could be detonated by the metal hulls of ships, and acoustic mines that could be triggered by the sound of a ship's engines.

On the ground, the British military made significant progress in improving the capabilities of its infantry units. One key innovation was the use of armoured personnel carriers, which allowed soldiers to move more quickly and securely across the battlefield. The British also made use of new types of small arms, including the STEN gun, a lightweight and reliable submachine gun that could be produced quickly and inexpensively. Originally designed in 1940 by Major R. V. Shepherd and Harold Turpin the Mark II STEN gun, which was produced during 1942 and 1943, was the most common variant. The name STEN is an acronym of the creators surnames along with 'EN' for the Enfield factory where the weapons were produced.

Soldiers with a Mk III Sten gun

In addition to these technological innovations, the British military also made significant strides in developing new tactics and strategies. For example, the British began to use specialised units, such as the Commandos, for tasks including amphibious landings and raids on enemy positions. The British also made extensive use of deception and disinformation tactics, using fake radio signals and other techniques to mislead the enemy about the location and strength of their forces.

United States of America

The U.S. Navy submarine USS Tang

As World War II raged, the battle under the ocean waves played an increasingly important role in both offensive and defensive operations. All sides were rapidly developing submarine technology to achieve naval dominance. In 1943 the US launched the first of its Balao-class submarines. It would go on to become their most successful submarine design with the launch of 120 boats. Thicker steel in both the hull and the pressure skins meant the Balao-class submarines could dive to a depth of 400 feet, a full 100 feet deeper than its predecessors. This extra depth allowed them to more easily evade attack from enemy destroyers. Although they had diesel engines on-board, these were used to generate electricity; the drive shaft and propulsion system was actually driven by an electric motor. Of the 120 Balao submarines that entered service only 9 were lost on active duty in the war. The fleet were devastating against the Japanese merchant fleet, all but destroying it. One submarine alone, the *USS Tang*, was responsible for sinking 33 ships. The *USS Archerfish* sank the Japanese aircraft carrier *Shinano* in 1944. It remains to this day the largest warship ever sunk by a submarine.

Another piece of American military hardware that also played a significant role in the war was the M4 Sherman tank. A simple design and the use of interchangeable parts made assembly quick and efficient. By 1943 mass production was in full swing with nearly 50,000 Shermans ultimately entering the battlefield. The turret-mounted 75mm main gun was effective against most Axis tanks, and the machine guns provided the tank with a good defence against infantry. The M4 Sherman was also known for its mobility and durability. It had a top speed of around 30mph and was able to cross trenches and other obstacles with ease. The tank was also relatively well-armoured, which helped protect the crew from enemy fire. The US supplied the UK over 17,000 Sherman tanks; all playing a valuable role in the liberation of Western Europe.

M4 Sherman production line in Warren, Michigan

Germany

In 1943, the German military continued to develop and improve its technology, although the tide of the war was beginning to turn against them. The German army had a strong tradition of technological innovation, and this continued even as their resources and manpower were stretched thin by the fighting on multiple fronts.

One area of focus for German military technology development in 1943 was in the field of tank design. The German army had been a pioneer in the development of armoured warfare, and they continued to work on improving their tanks. The Tiger I heavy tank was introduced in 1942, and it proved to be a formidable weapon on the battlefield. In 1943, work began on the development of the Tiger II, which would become one of the most heavily armed and armoured tanks of the war. It was powered by a 23-litre V12 petrol engine built by Maybach.

A Tiger II tank on the streets of Budapest

An Me 262A at the National Museum of the USAF

The Messerschmitt Me 262, which was the world's first operational jet-powered fighter aircraft, was also being developed and trialled in 1943. Despite its cutting-edge technology, the Me 262 faced significant production and logistical challenges that limited its impact on the war effort. These included an edict by Adolf Hitler in mid-1943 that the plane be configured as a fighter bomber as opposed to a defensive interceptor. Hitler's interference delayed the introduction of the Me 262 into service until April 1944.

The Henschel Hs 293 was a glide bomb that could be dropped from aircraft to attack ships and other land-based targets. Engineers at the German firm Henschel & Son started development in 1940. Its radio control technology was considered a significant innovation in guided missile technology. The first recorded use of the bomb in combat was on the 25th August 1943 in the Bay of Biscay against the Royal Navy ship, HMS Bideford. A Luftwaffe aircraft successfully guided the missile to strike the ship but the bomb didn't go off so only minor damage was caused. Two days later a squadron of German Dornier Do 217 aircraft attacked the 1st Support Group of Royal Navy ships also in the Bay of Biscay. One of the vessels, HMS Egret, was sunk with the loss of 198 lives. It was the first ship ever to be sunk by a guided missile.

An Hs 293 on display in the Udvar-Hazy Center

Russia

When Germany invaded in 1941, Russia pulled back its industrial production to the Ural Mountains, often dismantling factories piece by piece, transporting plant and machinery by train and then reassembling it. As Nazi forces encircled their major cities every effort was put into producing the means to fight back. During the war the Russians mass produced two of the most effective weapons the arena of war has ever seen: The Katyusha rocket launcher and the T-34 tank. The Katyusha is a multiple rocket launcher

Russian Katyusha rocket launchers

which was often loaded onto the back of Studebaker trucks provided by the Americans. When deployed they could lay waste to the battlefield and the howl they emitted struck fear into the enemy, leading them to be dubbed "Stalin's Organs." The Katyusha were cheap, plentiful and effective. Though highly inaccurate the sheer volume of their payload made them a very effective weapon. The largest launchers could deliver 72 missiles in one go. In 1942 they came into their own when the Russians mounted an assault against Nazi forces in their bid to retake the city of Stalingrad. The city was liberated in the spring of 1943.

1943 saw the peak of Russian tank production. By now the T-34 tank had proven itself on the battlefield due to being faster and more agile than existing German tank models. Production now reached 1,300 per month which equates to three full-strength tank divisions. These would be put to urgent use in the summer of 1943 during the Battle of Kursk - the largest tank battle in history. The battle was fought between German Tiger and Panther tanks against divisions of Soviet T-34 and KV-1 tanks in a region 400km south-west of Moscow. Despite the German's initial advantage, the Soviet's superior numbers and tactics ultimately led to their victory, effectively ending the German's offensive capabilities on the Eastern Front.

The T-34/76 tank

The Dambusters Raid

On the night of 16th May 1943, Wing Commander Guy Gibson led 617 Squadron of the Royal Air Force on an audacious bombing raid to destroy three dams in the Ruhr valley, the industrial heartland of Germany. The mission was code named 'Operation Chastise'. The dams were heavily protected. Torpedo nets stopped underwater attacks and anti-aircraft guns defended them against enemy bombardment. But 617 Squadron had a secret weapon: the 'bouncing bomb'. The Möhne dam in Germany's Ruhr valley helped provide water supply for much of the surrounding area. Water from its reservoir was also used to

Barnes Wallis watching trials

generate electricity. It was thought that destruction of this dam and others in the region would cause massive disruption to German war production. Plans for an attack had been considered as early as 1937, but it took until 1942 to develop a weapon capable of destroying them and the aircraft to deliver it. In 1942 the British engineer Barnes Wallis began working on plans for a bomb that could skip across water. He developed the idea by experimenting with bouncing marbles across a water tub in his back garden. Wallis thought the new weapon could be used

Guys Gibson's Lancaster with Upkeep under

to attack battleships in port, but research soon focused on using it against dams. The Admiralty and the RAF carried out extensive tests across the country. These revealed that the drum-shaped bomb (code name 'Upkeep') needed to be dropped from the height of 60ft and at a ground speed of 232mph. The bomb would spin backwards across the surface before reaching the dam. Its residual spin would then drive the bomb down the wall of the dam before exploding at its base. All that was needed now was men to fly specially modified Lancaster bombers which could carry the 'Upkeep'. In late March 1943, a new squadron was formed to carry out the raid.

Initially code named Squadron X, 617 was led by the 24-year-old Guy Gibson and was made up of air crew from Britain, Canada, the USA, Australia and New Zealand. With one month to go before the raid, and with only Gibson knowing the full details of the operation, the squadron began intensive training in low-level night flying and navigation. From 9.28pm on 16th May 1943, 133 aircrew in 19 Lancasters took off in three waves to bomb the dams. Gibson was flying in the first wave and his aircraft was the first to attack the Möhne at 12.28am, but five more aircraft had to drop their bombs before it breached. Other Lancasters attacked the Edersee, which collapsed at 1.52am. Meanwhile, aircraft from the two other waves bombed the Sorpe, but it remained intact. Of the 133 aircrew that took part, 53 men were killed and 3 were captured, On the ground, around 1,300 people were killed in the resulting flooding. Although the impact on industrial production was limited, the raid gave a significant morale boot to the people of Britain. The last surviving member of 617 squadron George Leonard Johnson, known as Johnny Johnson, died aged 101 on December 7th 2022.

The breached Möhne dam the day after the raids

The Warsaw Ghetto Uprising

The Warsaw Ghetto uprising of 1943 was the biggest act of civil defiance against the monstrous Nazi regime. In 1939 German authorities began to concentrate Poland's Jewish population of around 3 million into a number of crowded and squalid ghettos located in cities. The largest of which was the Warsaw Ghetto, which housed some 400,000 people in little over a square mile. On 22nd July 1942, the Jewish Council of Warsaw published a Nazi notice to the ghetto stating that almost all of its inhabitants would be deported to camps in the east, regardless of age or gender. Mass deportations began and by 12th

The resistance faced overwhelming power

September 1942 approximately 300,000 of the ghetto's inhabitants had been deported to the Treblinka extermination camp or murdered. Roughly 50,000 people remained in the ghetto. When the deportations halted in September, the utter despair felt by many Jews throughout the mass deportations hardened into growing a resistance. As the historian Emanuel Ringelblum, who was incarcerated in the ghetto, noted 'it seems to me that people will no longer go to the slaughter like lambs. They want the enemy to pay dearly for their lives. They'll

Forcibly pulled out from bunkers

fling themselves at them with knives, staves, coal gas...they'll not allowed themselves to be seized in the street, for they know that work camp means death these days'. Inhabitants of the ghetto had heard rumours of the extermination camps operating in the east, and many guessed what fate awaited them. Determined not to be taken to their deaths, preparations were made to resist the Germans should any more deportations take place. These preparations were led by a variety of resistance groups, such as the Jewish Combat Organisation and Jewish Military Union. At 6am on 18th January 1943, deportations from the ghetto were resumed. As the Germans began to gather Jews the remaining inhabitants in the ghetto surprised the Nazis by defying orders, hiding, and putting up an armed resistance. Several Nazi soldiers were injured, and, by 21st January, the deportations ceased. Between 5000 and 6500 Jews were taken to be deported to camps in the east. Following this resistance, Jews built bunkers and hideouts for a defensive battle, assuming that the Nazis would soon retaliate. They continued to collect weapons and bullets through connections with the Polish underground and prepared for an attack.

On 19th April 1943, the Nazis began their attack, led by SS General Jürgen Stroop. Within fifteen minutes, Jewish fighters retaliated, many with handmade weapons, initially forcing the German troops to retreat on the first day. The Nazis changed tack, and slowly destroyed the ghetto, building by building, forcing Jews remaining in hiding to appear or be killed. 27 days after the initial April attack, on 16th May, the uprising was crushed by the Nazis and the ghetto destroyed. The 42,000 survivors of the uprising were deported to concentration camps and extermination camps. While the uprising ultimately failed, it was an extremely significant display of resistance from Jews in Warsaw. It delayed the Germans' timeline of deportations and inspired other resistance movements across the German-occupied areas.

Captured Hehalutz fighters

The Victoria Cross

The Victoria Cross. the UK's highest military honour is awarded for acts of extreme bravery in the face of enemy fire. So far twenty-six VCs have been awarded to the brave fighting men of Nepal. Born in Barpak village in western Nepal, Gaje, a Gurung of the Ghale tribe, enlisted in the Indian army in 1934. Following training, he joined the 2nd battalion, 5th Royal Gurkha Rifles (Frontier Force), subsequently serving in Waziristan and in operations against that now-forgotten thorn in the side of the British Raj, the Fakir of Ipi. From 1939 to 1942, Gaje served as an instructor at the regimental depot in Abbotabad. In May 1943 Gaje Ghale was serving as a havildar (sergeant) with the 2nd battalion, 5th Royal Gurkha Rifles. This was during the 17th Indian Division's bitter and bloody struggle with the Japanese 33rd Division on the Tiddim Road in Burma, in the final phase of the Indian division's withdrawal through the Chin Hills. The Japanese occupied a crucial position on the Basha East Hill, the approach to which was a narrow ridge little more than 15 ft wide. Two attempts to take the position faltered in the face of withering fire from Japanese machine-gun nests and artillery and mortars

The Victoria Cross Medal

concealed in the jungle. On May 25th, Gaje, now in command of his company's D platoon, was ordered to take the position. Encouraging his riflemen and shouting the Gurkha's battle-cry "Ayo Gurkhali!" (the Gurkhas are upon you), Gaje attacked. Although badly wounded by a Japanese grenade, he led his men along the ridge and, apparently oblivious to the fire-power raining down, closed with the enemy in a bitter hand-to-hand fight. It was an action which won him the Victoria Cross, and as the citation put it, Gaje "dominated the fight" with "his outstanding example, dauntless courage and superb leadership. Hurling grenades and covered in blood from his own wounds, he led assault after assault." The young Gurkhas, "spurred on by the irresistible will of their leader to win, stormed and carried the hill by a magnificent effort and inflicted heavy casualties on the Japanese." Having gained the position, Gaje held it, despite continued

heavy fire, refusing to have his wounds dressed until ordered to do so by an officer. In 1944 the Viceroy of India, Field Marshal Lord Wavell, presented Gaje Ghale with his VC at an investiture at the Red Fort in Delhi before a crowd of more than 5,000. In 1946, Gaje paid the first of many visits to London, taking part in the victory parade. Granted the honorary rank of Captain, Gaje Ghale retained close links with former regimental colleagues and was a frequent and very welcome guest in Britain, regularly attending reunions of the Victoria Cross and George Cross Association. With other Gurkha VCs, he attended the opening of the Gurkha Museum at Winchester in 1990 and was present at ceremonies marking the 50th anniversary of VJ Day in London in 1995.

Major Gaje Ghale (pictured centre)

Field Marshal Lord Wavell presenting Gaje Ghale with his Victoria Cross medal in 1944

The Story of Seven US Presidents in WWII

John F. Kennedy was hoping to enter Yale Law School in 1940 but changed his mind when war seemed imminent. It wasn't easy for him to enlist in the military though as his lower back issues medically disqualified him. Alan Kirk, a friend of his father's, helped Kennedy join the U.S. Naval Reserve. In April 1943, Kennedy took command of PT-109, an 80-foot torpedo boat later rammed by a Japanese tanker. Kennedy bravely got his men to shore and was able to keep them alive through desperate efforts. The future President's heroism won him several honours, including the Navy and Marine Corps Medal and a Purple Heart. The story of Kennedy and his PT-109 formed a major part of the election campaign when he ran for President in 1960. When the Japanese attacked Pearl Harbor, Lyndon B. Johnson was already a congressman. A member of the Naval Reserves, Johnson was called into service just three days after the attack. This future President was close to President Roosevelt, and FDR assigned him to survey the conditions in the South-West Pacific. Johnson then served

John F. Kennedy on-board his PT-109 torpedo boat in 1943

under General Douglas MacArthur, overseeing bombing raids on New Guinea. When war broke out, Richard Nixon was working in the Office of Price Administration. His job in government and his Quaker faith would have granted him a draft deferral. Instead, he chose to apply to the Navy. The future President first acted as the Commander of Naval Air Station Ottumwa, Iowa. In 1941, Gerald Ford had recently graduated from law school and opened up a practice in Grand Rapids, Michigan. He enlisted in the Navy after the attack on Pearl Harbor. Ford ended up on the USS Monterey, which was commissioned from June 17th 1943 until December 1944. While he was aboard, the carrier participated in many actions in the Pacific War. Ronald Reagan was assigned to United States Army Air Forces, Public Relations. In this role, he starred in several training films made to improve troop

Captain Ronald Reagan at Fort Roach in 1943

Lyndon Baines Johnson in his naval uniform

readiness. While serving, he appeared in the 1943 film, *This Is the Army*, and helped promote war bonds to the general public. His active duty ended in December 1945, having reached the rank of Army Captain. George H.W. Bush grew up wealthy, the son of banker and politician Prescott Bush. Despite his social standing, this future President was eager to participate in WWII. He enlisted in the Navy the day he turned 18 and by the age of 19 he flew in his first combat mission, bombing the Japanese-held Wake Island. Unlike the other men on this list, Dwight D. Eisenhower had spent his entire life in the military when WWII came around. In fact, he is the only President to serve in both World Wars. In December 1943, Franklin Roosevelt declared Eisenhower the Supreme Allied Commander. The General oversaw the D-Day landings at Normandy, a major step towards winning the war. Soon after, the Allied Forces had liberated France and won victory in Europe. After the war, Eisenhower was so popular that he was advised to run for President. He took the advice and served two terms from 1953 to 1961.

George H.W. Bush

The Bethnal Green Station Tragedy

On the night of 3rd March, 1943, clusters of people were milling around outside the entrance to the station as they often did when expecting an air raid. They stood chatting, smoking and drinking tea. The air-raid siren sounded at 8.17pm and floods of people left nearby homes, pubs and cinemas to make their way to shelters. Within ten minutes, three buses had unloaded their passengers at the entrance to the station, drivers following instructions to drop passengers at the nearest shelter as soon as they heard a warning. When bombing was frequent, policemen were posted outside large shelters, but the comparative lack of raids by 1943 and a reduction in police numbers because of conscription meant that there had not been permanent police posts at shelter entrances since the summer of 1941. Because of blackout laws, the first staircase into the shelter was also poorly lit. There were 19 steps that led to a landing, after which there were seven more to the right going down to the booking hall and the escalators. There was no central railing to hold on

London Underground Stations were commonly used as air raid shelters during The Blitz

to. A woman with a child stumbled at the bottom of the steps and tripped over, pulling an elderly man on top of her. Before they could get to their feet, other people began falling on top of them and the crowd above, unable to see in the gloom, pressed on down the stairs, unaware of the horror unfolding below them. In a matter of seconds hundreds of people, five or six bodies deep, were piled on top of each other. In the stairwell at the bottom, the pile of bodies was five feet high. People couldn't move, pinned down by the weight of those above them. The pressure of the crush meant that chests could not expand sufficiently to breathe and within seconds most were unconscious. Wardens coming up from the booking hall found it almost impossible to extract people. A few babies were carried out and one or two people who were only partially trapped by their legs. Staff, rescue services and volunteers attempted to pull corpses and injured people from the top of the staircase. The darkness and the pressure made extricating

The stairs leading down were poorly lit due to blackout laws

people extremely slow, difficult work. It took more than three hours for the last casualty to be pulled out. Over the next few hours the true horror of the accident became clear: an unimaginable 173 people had lost their lives: 62 children, 84 women and 27 men. Over 90 people were injured, and although many were taken to local hospitals that night, others were too busy looking for their loved ones to be treated until days later. Astonishingly, one of the last to be removed was a seven-year-old girl who was not only alive, but walked down to the first-aid post unaided. It was the largest single loss of life in the UK during WWII not directly due to enemy action.

This plaque at the station remembers the victims

The Rescue of the Danish Jews

October 2nd 1943 is the day on which the government of Sweden announced its readiness to give safe haven to the entire Jewish population of neighbouring Denmark. In the weeks that followed, Sweden was able to fulfil that promise, after a mass effort on the part of both Danish officials and civilians led to the transport of most of Denmark's Jews across the Oresund Strait to safety. Denmark had been invaded by Nazi Germany on April 9th 1940. Because it was marginal to Germany's greater strategy and as they had only a small Jewish population, Denmark was subjected to a relatively gentle occupation, called by

Sailing the choppy waters to Ystad in Sweden

Germany a "model protectorate." Berlin sent under one hundred officials to Denmark, as compared with the 22,000 it sent to occupied France. The Danish government was permitted to remain in power as well, and the country's army was not disbanded. The Jewish community of Denmark numbered approximately 7,800 before the war and its members were for the most part well-integrated into society. For the first few years of occupation, Berlin was willing to tolerate Copenhagen's claim that the country had no "Jewish problem." But by the summer of 1943, there was a precipitous decline in German forbearance. By then, the war was going against the Nazis and members of the Danish resistance became bolder in their campaign against the occupiers. When the Germans demanded that the Danes crack down on the resistance, the local government refused. It also refused to accede to a diktat that it civil disobedience labour actions that followed several nationwide strikes. Instead, on August 29th , the Danish government resigned,. That same day, the Germans took direct control of administration and declared martial law. Georg Duckwitz, a German diplomat assigned to Copenhagen, tipped off members of the local resistance that the arrest of the Jews was imminent. The resistance passed the word on to the head of the Jewish community and the acting chief rabbi (the regular chief rabbi had been arrested several days earlier, together with some 100 other prominent Jews.) In the meantime, the Swedish Foreign Ministry, aware of the dangers facing Danish Jews, empowered its ambassador in Copenhagen to issue Swedish passports to them, an act that would pave the way for them to claim asylum in Sweden. On October 1st, Adolf Hitler gave the order for the rounding up of the Jews and on the following day Stockholm announced publicly that it was ready to take them all in. According to Yad Vashem (the World Holocaust Remembrance Center), some 7,200 Jews made the crossing to Sweden, while about 470 were arrested before they could escape into hiding. The latter were deported to Theresienstadt concentration camp, but even then, all but 70 survived until the war's end, in large part because of constant pressure from Denmark, which insisted successfully that its citizens be permitted to receive aid packages, and that they not be sent to death camps. There were also some 150 Jewish children whose parents left them behind with Christian families because they were considered too young to be evacuated.

Skipper Otto Andersen and his crew on-board the boat Gerda III ferried Jewish refugees ten at a time to Sweden. In all, they ferried 300 Jews to safety

RNLI Rescues

The Royal National Lifeboat Institution was founded by Sir William Hillary in 1824. Its motto "with courage nothing is impossible" was never more relevant than during the Second World War. Between 1939 and 1945 lifeboat crews saved 6,376 lives. This figure excludes the thousands of men rescued in the Dunkirk evacuation of 1940. Rescues were done without fear or favour and many enemy combatant lives were saved, leading some to criticise the Institution, believing that they should have been left to drown. The following are three of the many rescues that took place in 1943 alongside the rewards and compensation paid to the crews.

HARTLEPOOL, Co. DURHAM. At about 3pm in the afternoon of the 19th of September, 1943, the 18-tonne motor fishing boat Alexandra, with a crew of five, was fishing some 10 miles east-north-east of Heugh Light in Hartlepool Bay, when the men saw an object one and a half miles away. They slipped their gear and made for it, to find that it was a dinghy with three men of the Royal Canadian Air Force in it. They said that they had crashed a short time before and that a fourth man was in the water. The fishing boat searched and found him, but he was already dead from head injuries The rescuers were thanked by the R.A.F. station to which the aeroplane belonged. *Rewards: £5 and £1 for expenses.*

ISLE OF WHITHORN, WIGTOWNSHIRE. At 1pm in the afternoon of the 16th of August, 1943, the auxiliary rescue-boat, while out fishing with a crew of four, saw a small rowing boat in difficulties three-quarters of a mile from Stein Head Look-out. A light easterly wind was blowing, with a choppy sea. She went to the boat, found on board three engineers from Cairn Head military camp, who were exhausted, took the boat in tow and brought her to the Isle of Whithorn at 2.50pm. But for the timely help given, the rowing boat would have been carried away by the strong tide. *Rewards: £2 10s. and 4s. 2d. for fuel.*

Three engineers were in difficulty in a small rowing boat

SHERINGHAM, NORFOLK. At about 3:40pm in the afternoon of the 26th of July, 1943, an American B-17 Flying Fortress bombing aeroplane crashed into the sea about two miles north-by-east of Sheringham. The sea was calm, but the Fortress sank in seven minutes. The lifeboat crew were assembled, but meanwhile six men had set off in a motor fishing boat. They found the whole crew of ten American airmen, some in their rubber dinghy, others clinging to it, and rescued them. On their way back they met the lifeboat. *Rewards: £3 15s. ; and 2s. 3d. for fuel used.*

The B-17 similar to this crashed and sank in 7 minutes

Wojtek the Bear

In 1943 The People's Dispensary for Sick Animals (PDSA) Dickin Medal was instituted in the UK by animal welfare pioneer and social reformer Maria Dickin. It is the animal equivalent of the Victoria Cross. Made of bronze it carries the inscription "For Gallantry" and "We Also Serve" within a laurel wreath. The first medals were awarded to three carrier pigeons - White Vision, Winkie and Tyke - who delivered messages that contributed to the rescue of aircrew ditched in enemy occupied territory. There were many other tales of animal heroics during the

Wojtek sits in front of a soldier

war, but the one that best captured the public's imagination was the story of a remarkable bear. Corporal Wojtek Perski was a Syrian Brown Bear and a hero of World War II. In 1942, Wojtek was purchased by the 22nd Transport Company, Artillery Division, II Corps of the Polish Army in Iran. As a small cub, the soldiers fed Wojtek condensed milk from a bottle. As Wojtek grew up, he developed a taste for beer, wine, and cigarettes, which he would only chew if they were lit. He would also wrestle with his fellow soldiers and was truly one of the boys. Wojtek had his first brush with valour while still in Iran, when he captured a thief who had broken into an ammunition compound where he was sleeping. The ensuing commotion allowed the human soldiers to come and arrest the thief. As the 22nd Transport Company prepared to enter the war zone in Italy in 1943, the soldiers and Wojtek encountered a logistical problem. Animals were not allowed to accompany the army during conflict. To resolve this issue, the Company gave Wojtek a salary, an official rank of Private and a serial number. Wojtek became an enlisted soldier. The Polish II Corp was tasked with breaking the Nazi defences at Monte Cassino. During the conflict, Wojtek was at the artillery firing line and was seen moving crates of ammunition from the trucks to the cannon lines. He was not put off by the sound of shellfire. The Poles were successful in taking the Nazi stronghold. After the battle, Wojtek was promoted to Corporal. The 22nd Transport Company was also permitted to change their official badge to a silhouette of Wojtek holding an artillery shell. On November 15th 1947, with the war over, Wojtek was given to Edinburgh Zoo where he became a huge attraction and lived out the rest of his days in peace. Wojtek died in December 1963 at the age of 21 which, given his frequent scrapes with death and his liking for cigarettes, was a ripe old age. A bronze statue of the heroic bear alongside a polish soldier was unveiled in 2015 and sits beneath Edinburgh Castle. He is also fondly remembered in Poland and a memorial entirely funded by public donation stands in Krakow.

After the war Wojtek lived the rest of his life in Edinburgh Zoo where he was a frequent guest on the BBC children's programme Blue Peter

George Orwell once said that sport was "war minus the shooting", but in 1943 war made sport almost irrelevant. Sport in Britain had virtually shut down and that which was played was mainly to boost morale. There was no Wimbledon Tennis Championship, the centre court had even taken a direct hit in 1940. The French Open Tennis tournament was the only one of the "Big Four" to take place. However, as the championship was played under Nazi control the results were voided after the war. Official football, rugby and cricket leagues were suspended. Horse racing continued, but only in areas away from our major towns and cities. Wartime leagues were set up in both rugby and association football. Sports men and women had signed up for the services. When they returned on leave many would turn out for a team they were stationed

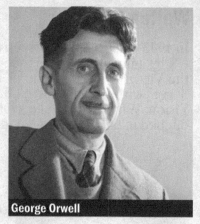

George Orwell

near which gave a lot of people the chance to see their idols in the flesh for the first time. Women's football thrived as factory teams were set up, though no official leagues were formed. The arrival of American GIs meant that British people saw for the first time sports that were alien to them, although baseball and basketball did look a lot like rounders and netball. Many sports women and men lost the best years of their lives, or worse still lost their lives, during the war. One of the greatest sportsmen ever, cricketer Don Bradman, joined the Australian army and suffered an injury in

A women's football match on a snow covered pitch in Fallowfield

training. Medical examination showed that he had poor eyesight, remarkable for a man who averaged nearly a hundred with the bat. The war impinged on sport in many different ways: Leigh rugby league team had to abandon their ground when a neighbouring cable factory needed to expand. The Olympics that were due to be held in Tokyo in 1940 were abandoned and would remain dormant until 1948 when war-ravaged London hosted the games. Even in countries untouched directly by the destruction of war, sport was seen as an unnecessary distraction. Though the American mainland was not directly threatened, many sports were seen as frivolous in a time of great national crisis and many sports stars either enlisted or turned their efforts to fundraising for the war.

Don Bradman

Association Football: The 1943 football season in England was greatly affected by World War II, which was raging on at the time. Many players were called up to serve in the military, and as a result, football leagues and cup competitions were suspended or postponed. Despite these challenges, efforts were made to keep the sport going during the war years. The Football League, which was the top professional league in England, did not hold a full season in 1943. Instead, regional leagues and cup competitions were organised. One of these was the Football League War Cup, also known as the Football League North and South Cup. It was contested by teams in the North and South regional leagues, with the final being held in London. League South was won by Arsenal and League North by Blackpool so they met in the final where Blackpool beat Arsenal 4-2 at Chelsea's Stamford Bridge in

Goalkeepers commonly wore flat caps

front of a crowd over 55,000. League West was won by Lovell's Athletic F.C., the staff team of a sweet factory from Newport, Wales. These tournaments provided some much needed entertainment and distraction for the public during a difficult and uncertain time. Despite the disruptions caused by the war, football remained a popular and beloved sport in England. Many people turned out to watch the matches, and the competitions provided a sense of normality and continuity during a time of great upheaval.

The 1943 football season may not have been a typical one, but it was still an important part of the country's sporting history.

A British Army team walk out to start a match in Rome

North of the border in Scotland there were similar moves to keep the spirits up by providing much needed sporting entertainment. The Southern Football League 1942-3 was won by Rangers, with Morton second. Celtic could only finish ninth. The Southern League Cup was played in a four group format with the winners progressing to the semi-finals. Rangers, Falkirk, Hamilton Academical and Third Lanark all made it through. Rangers fought out a 1-1 draw with Falkirk in the final, but were awarded the Cup by dint of the fact that they won more corners (11-3). Falkirk were represented at centre half by Bob Shankly, elder brother of legendary Liverpool manager Bill. None of the records either side of the border were recognised by the respective Football Association, much to the annoyance of Rangers fans whose team won five "wartime cups".

A flying header beats the goalkeeper

Sport
Rugby

Rugby League

The 1942-43 season began on Saturday 5th September 1942. As in the previous season, there were still only the three Lancashire clubs who had not had to close down and withdraw from the League. The Northern Rugby League continued with a single 14 club competition. As the clubs played a different number of matches, the league positions and the title would be decided on a percentage basis. At the completion of the regular season Wigan were on top of the league with a percentage success of 81.25% whilst Dewsbury were a close second on 78.12%. Although Bradford Northern won more games than anyone else, their percentage success was only 73.80%, and consequently they finished third. St. Helens finished 14th out of the 14 clubs with only 2 wins from 15. Dewsbury went on to defeat Halifax 33–16 on aggregate in the play-off final and win the Championship for the second consecutive season. However, the Championship was declared null and void as Dewsbury had fielded an ineligible player in the semi-final, which seemed a bit harsh given the circumstances. The Wartime Emergency Leagues did not count as an official league championship. In the Rugby League Challenge Cup, Dewsbury beat Leeds 16–15 on aggregate over two legs in front of a total crowd of 26,470. With the Lancashire League suspended, Wigan competed in the Yorkshire Cup. The trophy was won by Dewsbury who beat Huddersfield 7–2 on aggregate in two low scoring encounters.

Rugby Union

Rugby Union was run by the Rugby Football Union and during the war they relaxed their previous ban on Rugby League players taking part in Union. Rugby at the time was class based, Union players were typically upper class, public school educated whilst League players were traditionally working class. A series of internationals was arranged, but most intriguing of all, two Union vs League matches were played. Even though they were held under Union rules, the League players won both games. It was something that would be talked about in the Working Men's Clubs of the north for many years to come. In France, the battle between League and Union extended far beyond the rugby pitch and lasted many years after the war. After the fall of France, the French Rugby Union worked with the Nazi occupiers to have their game sanctioned and Rugby League banned. Even though the ban was lifted after the war, Rugby League was barred from using the term rugby until the mid-1980s, instead having to refer to themselves as Jeu à Treize- the game of thirteen. Rugby Union is played with fifteen players per side.

Stade Bordelais v US Dax at Parc des Princes during WWII

Cricket

That Wisden, the cricket lovers' bible, should appear in 1943 was a triumph of hope over experience. There was little to report. The County Championship in Britain was suspended and there was no Sheffield Shield in Australia. This most British of sports was put on hold except for a few Army vs Navy games at the home of cricket, Lords. London's other main venue, The Oval, had been converted into a prisoner-of-war camp, though it was never used as such. In 1939 there was a planned England tour of India which was abandoned at the outbreak of war. The fact that many of the cricketers were good team players served them well during the war. Here is a selection of the squad, highlighting their war records. Tragically one was to die and others missed their chance of ever playing for England.

A J Holmes *Right handed batsman for Sussex*

Flight Lieutenant in the RAF.

H T Bartlett *Left handed batsman for Sussex*

Joined the Royal Kent Regiment and served at the Normandy landings.

H Gimblett *Right handed batsman for Somerset*

Joined the Fire Service and helped to put out fires in the badly bombed ports of Plymouth and Bristol.

R H Human *Right handed batsman for Worcestershire*

Human was to go to India, not as a cricketer, but as a soldier with the Ox and Bucks Light Infantry. He died there on active service in November 1942, aged just 33.

R E S Wyatt *Right handed batsman for Warwickshire*

Served with distinction in the RAF.

S C Griffith *Right handed batsman for Sussex*

Served as second-in-command of the 6th Airborne Division for which he won the Distinguished Flying Cross.

T P B Smith *Spin bowler for Essex*

Served as a staff sergeant with the Essex Regiment in Alexandria, Egypt.

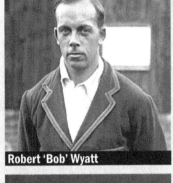

Robert 'Bob' Wyatt

Harold Gimblett

With so many men from the Empire stationed in Britain, there was ample scope for friendly cricket matches. Very often these were friendly in name only and were fiercely competitive. A drawn one-day match at Lord's between an England XI and a West Indies XI featured the young Alec Bedser and Trevor Bailey. Bedser made his mark by taking 6/27 in the West Indies first innings. In the drawn Sir PF Warner's XI v Royal Australian Air Force match at Lord's, Keith Miller top-scored in the RAAF's first innings, with 45 out of 100, as well as taking 2/20. The RAAF won a two-day match against The South at Hove by ten wickets. A strong England XI beat The Dominions by 8 runs in a two-day match at Lord's. Les Ames made 133 in the England first innings whilst Denis Compton then took 6/15 in eight overs. In their second innings, The Dominions came close to snatching an unlikely victory, with Stewie Dempster making 113.

Overview

Horse racing in the United Kingdom was greatly curtailed in 1943. There was no Grand National and no Royal Ascot. The Cheltenham Gold Cup, which had taken place a year earlier, was cancelled in both 1943 and 1944.

Ascot racecourse was turned into a German refugee camp, Epsom Downs (the traditional home of the Derby) was used for an anti-aircraft battery as it was handily situated close to London. Haydock Park became the first port of call for incoming French sailors and Nottingham housed the 7th Leicestershire Regiment. Even those racecourses that were not pressed into direct service were often ploughed for food production. These included Cartmel and Fakenham.

Nottingham racecourse was used by the army

The Derby

The main flat race of this or any year, the Derby, took place not in its traditional home, but at Newmarket. This so-called New Derby Stakes, was run on Saturday 19th June. It was won by *Straight Deal*. The winner was ridden by Tommy Carey, trained by Walter Nightingall and owned and bred by Dorothy Paget. The winning owner won a first prize of £4,388. The victory was by a short head and is the third fastest Derby in history.

In fact, the five fastest times in the classic were all recorded during the war, but these records do not count as Newmarket does not have the undulations of Epsom.

Straight Deal Derby 1943   Jockey
Churchill 'A' Series   T. H. Carey
Straight Deal, The New Derby Stakes winner

Racing in Ireland

Racing in neutral Ireland continued relatively unaffected by the war. This presented a problem for the authorities on both sides of the Irish Sea as it provided a regular and available betting market. The problem was compounded by the fact that gambling was illegal in Britain except at greyhound and horse tracks. Given that nearly of these were closed, the gambling market went underground. Illicit gaming houses, masquerading as clubs, and illegal betting began to spring up everywhere. In London alone, in 1943, police raided over a hundred of these joints.

Overview

Outside of a few college events in the USA and some non-recognised events in Nazi-controlled Europe, athletics virtually ground to a halt. The Olympics that had been scheduled to take place in Tokyo in 1940 were cancelled. The showpiece event would not return until London hosted the games in 1948. Instead we spotlight the lives of three athletes whose careers were affected by the war.

Louis Zamperini | American distance runner

Louis Zamperini

Zamperini ran in the 1936 Berlin Olympics and was training to take part in the Tokyo games, which were cancelled when war broke out. Zamperini enlisted and joined the US Army Air Corps as a bombardier. His plane was shot down near Japan and after 47 days drifting at sea on a raft, he and his fellow crew members were taken prisoner of war. They were subjected to horrendous treatment by their Japanese captors. By the time of his release at the end of the war, Zamperini's athletics career was over. He took to hard drinking but found religion and so began a healing process. Some of his torturers received forgiveness in person in 1950, when he visited them in prison in Tokyo. In 1998 Zamperini returned to Japan once again to carry the torch at the Nagano Winter Games.

Foy Draper | American Olympic champion sprinter

Foy Draper was an American athlete who won a gold medal in 4 × 100m Relay, alongside the great Jesse Owens, at the Berlin Olympics of 1936. He also reportedly held the world record for the 100-yard dash in a time of 9.4 seconds. This was all the more remarkable as he stood only 5'5" tall. During World War II, he served as a pilot in a twin-engine attack bomber A-208B "Havoc" in North Africa. Draper took off to take part in the battle of Kassarine Pass, Tunisia. He and his two crewmen never returned and they were officially declared dead on February 1st. His body was found and he is buried in the North African Cemetery and Memorial. His gravestone shows 4th January 1943 as the date of his death.

William Roberts | English sprinter

William "Bill" Roberts was an English sprinter who won a gold medal in the 4x400m relay event at the 1936 Summer Olympics in Berlin. He had further success in 1938 in the 440yd event at the British Empire games in Sydney, Australia. In Britain many athletes were enlisted to impart their knowledge of physical training to the armed forces, others saw active service. When war broke out Bill joined the RAF, in which he served with distinction. After the war he was able to resume his athletics career and captained the British team at the 1948 Olympic games in London.

Rocky Marciano - A legend born in South Wales

Rocky Marciano, born Rocco Francis Marchegiano, dropped out of high school after tenth grade to work and help support his family in a variety of jobs – washing dishes, gardening and working in a shoe factory. On 4th March 1943, at the age of 20, Rocky enlisted in the US Army in Boston. Marciano was assigned to the 150th Combat Engineers in Swansea, South Wales where he worked ferrying supplies across the English Channel to Normandy. Although there is very limited information to be found about his time in the army, it has been established that he first took up boxing in the service, reportedly as a way to avoid kitchen duties. One famous fight that would pass into local folklore was against future Welsh rugby captain Jack Matthews. The unofficial **Rocky Marciano** amateur contest would end in a draw, allowing Matthews to dine out on the story for years to come. While awaiting discharge, Marciano, representing the army, won the 1946 Amateur Armed Forces boxing tournament. After the war ended, he completed his service in March 1946 at Fort Lewis, Washington where he received an honourable discharge from the army. He returned home to Brockton, Massachusetts and continued to box as an amateur, pausing briefly to pursue a baseball career. He then returned to boxing and became the professional World Heavyweight Champion. He finished his career in 1955 undefeated with 49 wins, 43 by knockout.

Raging Bull vs Sugar Ray II - 5th February 1943

A rivalry is not a rivalry after just one fight. Ray Robinson and Jake LaMotta (nicknamed "Raging Bull") had faced each other for the very first time just four months prior at Madison Square Garden in New York. While both were world-rated and regarded as exceptional talents, it was the welterweight Robinson who impressed in their 1942 meeting. Jake won, at best, two rounds, as Sugar Ray used his speed and skills to take a one-sided decision win with relative ease. But both fighters preferred to stay busy and their first match had done brisk business. Robinson was already a high-profile contender, commanding big purses and big crowds, as the story was that he had not lost a match in some 125 consecutive fights, amateur and pro. This time Jake and Ray locked horns in Detroit, Robinson's hometown, in front of a sell-out Olympia Stadium. They were treated to a contest between an incredibly tough middleweight grinder and the gifted welterweight with the lightning-quick hands. After seven rounds it appeared Robinson had a commanding points lead and was on his way to another clear cut win. But then a desperate LaMotta dramatically came to life and began to railroad his man, applying relentless pressure and doing damage on the inside. No doubt those extra pounds came in handy for Jake as he manoeuvred his way past Robinson's reach and landed heavy shots. Starting in the eighth, it was all LaMotta and at the end of the round a right to the body followed by a vicious left hook to the head sent Sugar Ray through the ropes. He never did beat the count; the bell rang to save Robinson from what looked to some like an almost certain knockout loss. Sugar Ray then survived the last two rounds, but Jake remained in charge, battering his man and sealing an historic victory.

The Masters and Bobby Jones

When America entered the war, it was only natural that many annual sporting events were sacrificed in the name of national service. The Masters Tournament, annually held at Augusta, was no exception. Bobby Jones, who co-founded the Augusta tournament, pondered whether or not to go forward with the 1942 tournament. It was held and the tournament was won by Byron Nelson in a play-off against Ben Hogan. Immediately afterwards, Augusta was shut down as a golf club and the grounds were turned over to raising cattle and turkeys. The turkey operation was successful, but the cattle herd was something of a failure. The cattle not only destroyed many of the famous azaleas and camellias, they also ate the bark of many of the young trees. At the time of Pearl Harbour, Bobby Jones was almost 40 years old and thought too old to serve but he proved all his detractors wrong. He approached the Army Air Service for a commission, and he was enlisted with the rank of captain,

The 10th Hole "Camellia" at Augusta

in June 1942. His progression through the ranks was steady and in March 1943 he was promoted to major. In the same year, he was transferred to Military Intelligence with the Ninth Air Force and he sailed for England. In June 1944 he went out with the invasion force in the D-Day Landings. General Dwight D. Eisenhower who commanded the invasion force, would later go on to become the American President and also a member at Augusta.

Richmond Golf Club's Temporary Wartime Rules

Early in the war, bombs dropped on Richmond Golf Club. This led the members to create a set of tongue-in-cheek wartime rules in defiance of Nazi aggression. They became world famous and even led to Hitler's Minister of Propaganda to mention them in a broadcast.

1. Players are asked to collect the bomb and shrapnel splinters to save these causing damage to the mowing machines.
2. In competition, during gunfire or while bombs are falling, players may take shelter without penalty or ceasing play.
3. The positions of known delayed action bombs are marked by red flags at a reasonable, but not guaranteed, safe distance therefrom.
4. Shrapnel and/or bomb splinters on the fairways or in bunkers within a club's length of a ball may be moved without penalty, and no penalty shall be incurred if a ball is thereby caused to move accidentally.
5. A ball moved by enemy action may be replaced or, if lost or destroyed, a ball may be dropped not nearer the hole without penalty.
6. A ball lying in a crater may be lifted and dropped not nearer the hole, preserving the line to the hole, without penalty.
7. A player whose stroke is affected by the simultaneous explosion of a bomb may play another ball. Penalty one stroke.

Photo Credits

Credits shown in the order in which they appear in the book. Photos not listed are in the public domain.

Key to page numbers

fc = front cover; **ifc** = inside front cover; **tp** = title page; **cp** = contents page; **ap1** = acknowledgements page 1; **ap2** = acknowledgements page 2; **rop** = reader offer page; **ibc** = inside back cover; **bc** = back cover; **3** = page 3; **4** = page 4; etc.

Key to object position on page

tl = top left; *t* = top; *tc* = top centre; *tr* = top right; *cla* = centre left above; *ca* = centre above; *cra* = centre right above; *cl* = centre left; *c* = centre; *cr* = centre right; *clb* = centre left below; *cb* = centre below; *crb* = centre right below; *bl* = bottom left; *b* = bottom; *bc* = bottom centre; *br* = bottom right; *w* = whole page; *h* = header; *tb* = text background

Key to image licence types

CC BY-SA 2.0 = https://creativecommons.org/licenses/by-sa/2.0/deed.en;
CC BY-SA 3.0 = https://creativecommons.org/licenses/by-sa/3.0/deed.en;
CC BY-SA 4.0 = https://creativecommons.org/licenses/by-sa/4.0/deed.en;
(m) = image has been modified as permitted under licensing terms

fc *tc*: Queen Elizabeth II (m) © Yousuf Karsh, Wikimedia Commons, CC BY-SA 3.0; **fc** *bc*: Diplomats on bus (m) © FORTEPAN / Archiv für Zeitgeschichte ETH Zürich / Agnes Hirschi, Wikimedia Commons, CC BY-SA 3.0; **tp** *w*: Spitfire (m) © Richard Gosler, Unsplash; **2** *tr*: Playing piano, © Esko Manninen / Finnish Army, Wikimedia Commons, CC BY-SA 4.0; **5** *cla*: Edersee Dam, © Bundesarchiv, Bild 183-C0212-0043-012, Wikimedia Commons, CC BY-SA 3.0; **20** *cla*: Tony Blackburn © Featureflash Photo Agency / Shutterstock.com; **21** *clb*: Eric Idle © PythonProfessor, Wikimedia Commons, CC BY-SA 4.0; **22** *cla*: Michael Palin © The National Churches Trust, Wikimedia Commons, CC BY-SA 2.0; **22** *clb*: Cilla Black © Joost Evers / Anefo, Wikimedia Commons, CC BY-SA 3.0; **23** *cla*: Arthur Ashe © Los Angeles Times / UCLA Library, Wikimedia Commons, CC BY-SA 4.0; **23** *clb*: Robert De Niro © David Shankbone, Wikimedia Commons, CC BY-SA 3.0; **24** *tl*: Mick Jagger © Georges Biard, Wikimedia Commons, CC BY-SA 3.0; **24** *br*: Keith Richards © Raph_PH, Wikimedia Commons, CC BY-SA 2.0; **25** *clb*: Billie Jean King © Jonathan Exley, Wikimedia Commons, CC BY-SA 3.0; **26** *clb*: Keith Floyd © Dave Edwards / BBC Archive; **27** *cla*: Sir Ben Kingsley © Gage Skidmore, Wikimedia Commons, CC BY-SA 3.0; **27** *cb row 1*: Joe Pesci © yausser, Wikimedia Commons, CC BY-SA 2.0; **27** *crb row 1*: Graeme Garden © Andy, Flickr, CC BY-SA 2.0; **27** *cb row 2*: Tony Christie © Frank Schwichtenberg, Wikimedia Commons, CC BY-SA 3.0; **27** *crb row 2*: Malcolm McDowell © Georges Biard, Wikimedia Commons, CC BY-SA 3.0; **27** *crb row 3*: Roger Waters © Daigo Oliva, Wikimedia Commons, CC BY-SA 2.0; **27** *clb row 4*: Gloria Gaynor © Thomas Rodenbücher, Wikimedia Commons, CC BY-SA 2.0; **27** *cb row 4*: Chevy Chase © Alan Light, Wikimedia Commons, CC BY-SA 2.0; **27** *cb row 5*: Chas Hodges © Andrew D. Hurley, Wikimedia Commons, CC BY-SA 4.0; **31** *tl*: Coins © Jo Smiley Hailey, Unsplash.com; **31** *tr*: House © Sludgegulper, Wikimedia Commons, CC BY-SA 2.0; **31** *bl*: Radio © Auckland Museum, Wikimedia Commons, CC BY-SA 4.0; **31** *bc*: Bread © Dmitry Makeev, Wikimedia Commons, CC BY-SA 4.0; **31** *br*: Eggs © George Chernilevsky, Wikimedia Commons, CC BY-SA 4.0; **32** *tr*: Drilling Components © State Library of South Australia, Wikimedia Commons, CC BY-SA 2.0; **35** *tr*: RMS Cameronia © Alan Burnett, Flickr, CC BY-SA 2.0; **38** *ca*: Woolton Pie (m) © autumnroseuk, Wikimedia Commons, CC BY-SA 2.0; **39** *ca*: Carrot Cake (m) © Veganbaking.net from USA, Wikimedia Commons, CC BY-SA 2.0; **40** *cra*: Arthur's Seat (m) © Ad Meskens, Wikimedia Commons, CC BY-SA 3.0; **40** *crb*: Blackpool Tower (m) © Mike Peel, Wikimedia Commons, CC BY-SA 3.0; **46** *br*: The National Gallery (m) © Uukgoblin, Wikimedia Commons, CC BY-SA 3.0; **49** *clb*: Vera Lynn © Eric Koch / Anefo, Wikimedia Commons, CC BY-SA 3.0; **51** *tl*: Desert Island (m) © Pedro Monteiro, Unsplash.com; **55** *clb*: The Royal Albert Hall © Diliff, Wikimedia Commons, CC BY-SA 3.0; **56** *cl*: T.S.Eliot © Ellie Koczela, Wikimedia Commons, CC BY-SA 4.0; **57** *tl* & **57** *cl* & **58** *tl* & **58** *bl* & **59** *tl* & **59** *cl* & **59** *bl*: Created with the assistance of DALL·E 2; **62** *clb*: Noele Gordon © The Noele Gordon Archive @ www.noelegordon.co.uk; **64** *cb*: Clouds (m) © Billy Huynh, Unsplash.com; **66** *cla*: Drum Kidney Dialysis Machine © Werner Groß, Wikimedia Commons, CC BY-SA 3.0; **66** *clb*: Vulcan Bomber © RAF, Wikimedia Commons, CC BY-SA 1.0; **67** *clb*: Slinky © Roger McLassus, Wikimedia Commons, CC BY-SA 3.0; **72** *cra*: Tiger II tank © Bundesarchiv, Bild 101I-680-8282A-06 / Faupel, Wikimedia Commons, CC BY-SA 3.0; **73** *cra*: Rocket Launchers © RIA Novosti archive, image #303890 / Zelma, Wikimedia Commons, CC BY-SA 2.0; **78** *cl*: Stairs © Jan Baborák, Unsplash.com; **78** *br*: Memorial Plaque © Sunil060902, Wikimedia Commons, CC BY-SA 3.0; **79** *tr*: Boat with Jews sailing from Falster (Denmark) to Ystad in Sweden © National Museum of Denmark, Wikimedia Commons, CC BY-SA 2.0; **79** *bl*: Gerda III vessel © Ad Meskens, Wikimedia Commons, CC BY-SA 3.0; **80** *br*: B-17 Bomber © Airwolfhound, Wikimedia Commons, CC BY-SA 2.0; **82** *tr*: George Orwell © Cassowary Colorizations, Wikimedia Commons, CC BY-SA 2.0; **82** *br*: Don Bradman © Licensed-PD-Art, Wikimedia Commons, CC BY-SA 4.0; **86** *tr*: Racecourse Rails © Alan Murray-Rust, Wikimedia Commons, CC BY-SA 2.0; **86** *cr*: Straight Deal, with thanks to John Slusar, www.greyhoundderby.com; **93** *w*: Sailor Beware © John Philip Falter, Boston Public Library, Wikimedia Commons, CC BY-SA 2.0; **98** *tc*: Coffee Table (m) © Sincerely Media, Unsplash.com;

Graphic and Background Image Credits

Credits shown in the order in which they appear in the book.

Additional Key

(ic) = icon; (ph) = photo

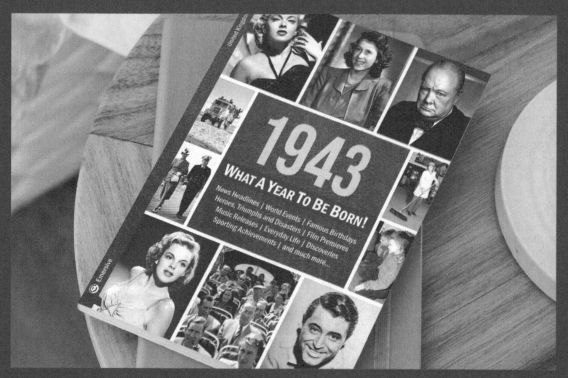

Join us for news on our future releases, reader promotions and behind-the-scenes content. All at:

www.subscribepage.com/join1943

It's completely free to join. As a subscriber, we will email you no more than once or twice a month. We will never share your email address and you can unsubscribe at any time.

Key to Front Cover Images

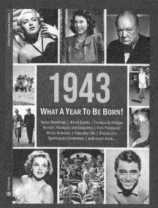

Clockwise from top left corner:
1. Actress Lana Turner (born in this year)
2. Queen Elizabeth II
3. Prime Minister Winston Churchill
4. Sweeping the platform at Earl's Court underground station
5. Evacuated children playing
6. Actor Cary Grant
7. Swiss diplomats travelling on an open top bus
8. Actress and Singer Judy Garland
9. Crown Princess Mountbatten visits the Swedish fleet
10. British Army troops advancing towards Tripoli